Praise for
Google Apps for Littles

"*Google Apps for Littles* is jam packed with practical and innovative ideas and projects you can use with your Littles tomorrow! This book truly shows the capabilities of not just technology but also of the students we teach."

—**Eric Curts**, ControlAltAchieve.com

"Inside this book, created by the dynamic duo of Alice Keeler and Christine Pinto, you will find nothing short of transformation. By believing that all of our Littles can, we can give our youngest learners powerful, student-centered, learning experiences. This book is loaded with practical, use-tomorrow lesson ideas, learning activities powered by G Suite, and proven strategies that will not only help transform elementary classrooms but also open your mind to what's possible in K–12 education. No matter what grade you teach, you will gain new ideas and insight by reading this book. Add this book to your reading list now!"

—**Kasey Bell**, ShakeUpLearning.com

"Christine and Alice provide both inspiration and practical application to empower our littlest learners in using technology. *Google Apps for Littles* is a must-have handbook for every primary educator to support them in creating creative, critical thinkers in a fun and forward-thinking way."

—**Cori Orlando**, TOSA at Simi Institute

"You've been nervous about using technology with Littles; it's always changing, it's overwhelming, and it creates a 'where do I begin' tornado of concerns. Look no further! Pinto and Keeler have made this super simple! I love this all-encompassing guide to support teachers and students. Awesome!"

—**Lavonna Roth**, creator and founder of Ignite Your S.H.I.N.E.®

D1404208

Google Apps for Littles

Believe They Can

Christine Pinto   **Alice Keeler**

Foreword by Michelle Baldwin

Published by Dave Burgess Consulting, Inc.
San Diego, CA
DaveBurgessConsulting.com

Cover Design by Genesis Kohler
Interior Design by My Writers' Connection

Library of Congress Control Number: 2017947006
Paperback ISBN: 978-1-946444-44-8
eBook ISBN: 978-1-946444-45-5
First Printing: February 2018

Contents

Foreword by Michelle Baldwin ix

Empowering Littles xi
    Meaningful Tech Integration xii

Chapter 1: Behind the Scenes 1
    Getting Set Up 1
        Email 2
        The Login Process 3
        Login Cards 4
        Profile Pictures 5

    Let's Get Started 6

Chapter 2: Technology Integration with Littles 7
    Device Handling and Digital Citizenship 8
    Create a Workflow 9
        A Chromebook Walk in Pinto's Classroom 10

    Choose a Seating Arrangement 10
        Center Rotations 10
        Gather on the Carpet 11
        Arrange Workspaces for Collaboration 12

    Google Apps for Multiple Devices 12
        Chromebook Users 13
        PC Users 14
        iPad or Tablet Users 15

Chapter 3: Explore Google Classroom 18
    Choose a Simple Class Title 19
    Title Assignments with a Hashtag and Number 19
    Put Frequently Used Sites in the About Tab 20
    Add Topics 21
    Parent Corner 22
    Nondigital 23
    Private Comments for Observations 24

    Sample Assignments 25
    Non-Google Classroom Users 26

Chapter 4: Activities Littles Can Do 27
    Create Drawings 27

Word Collage 28

Upgrade to Google Slides 29

Make Arrangements 30

Voice Typing 31

Pixel Art 33

Write Their Names 35

Check Their Spelling 37

Master Control-Z 38

Restore a File 39

Search Images with Word Families 39

Create All About Me Slides 42

Scavenger Hunts 44

Chapter 5: Collaborative Awesomeness 46

Collaborative Slides 47

Assigning Collaborative Docs to Groups 50

Group Docs Maker 51

Collaborate with Upper-Grade Students 53

Collaborate in Google Sheets 54

DiscussionTab 54

TemplateTab 56

Collaborate in a HyperDoc 58

Breakout EDU 61

Oompa Loompa Breakout EDU—Pinto Style 62

Chapter 6: Graphing in Google Sheets 63

Combine Technology and Manipulatives 64

Graph the Weather 64

A Step Further 65

Create Your Own Weather Chart 66

Manipulate a Google Drawing 66

Create Pie Charts 68

Chapter 7: Tech Tools to Support ELA 70

Google Classroom Private Comments 70

Google Keep 72

Draw Your Vocab 72

Google Docs 73

Draftback 74

Brainstorming Race 74

Read&Write 75

Fluency Tutor 76

Sequence Writing and Sundae Building 78

Magnetic Poetry 79

Storyboarding 79

Go Beyond the Basics 81

Map It Out 81

    Collaborative Maps 83

    Sharing a My Maps 84

Chapter 8: Tech Resources to Support Mathematics 85

Clearly Communicate Ideas 85

    Share Your Strategy Template 86

Faster Feedback 87

Using a Spreadsheet for
Immediate Feedback 88

    Check My Answer Template 89

    Digital Feedback 90

Models and Equations Activities 91

Sorting Shapes 92

Composite 2D Shapes 94

    Class Chat on Composite Shapes 94

Polyline Tool Activity 95

Partner Activity on Composite Shapes 97

Reason with Shapes 100

House Hunters 101

Math Puzzles 103

Chapter 9: Personalizing Feedback 105

Accessing Student Work 105

    Drive20 106

Bitmoji in Google Apps 106

    Bitmoji in Slides and
    Drawings 107

    Bitmoji in Docs 107

    Bitmoji in Forms 108

Webcam Feedback 109

    Screencast Video Feedback 109

Chapter 10: G Suite for Teachers 111
   1. Create a Place for Collaboration 111
      Team Drive 112
   2. Collaborate on Lesson Planning 112
      Notifications 114
      Comment and Suggestion Modes 114
   3. Create a Weekly Newsletter 115
      Title Your Document 115
      Create Headings 116
      Share Past Newsletters 116
   4. Create a Classroom Volunteer Form .118
   5. Create Thinking Maps 120
   6. Create a Class Roster 123
   7. Tools for Publishing 125
      Anyone Can View 125
      Publish to the Web 126
      ePubs 126

Conclusion 127

Thank You … 128

More from Dave Burgess Consulting, Inc. 129

About the Authors 139

Foreword
by Michelle Baldwin

One of the most wonderful things about teaching Littles is their insatiable curiosity. They look around with wonder-filled eyes and ask question after question, all the while skipping from one thing to the next to try to make sense of their world. I'm often envious watching my students in the blissful midst of a brand new experience, observing objects around them as things yet to be categorized and labeled. With their vivid imaginations, my students transform everyday, ordinary objects—rulers, jump ropes, building blocks, and anything else in their path—into entire cities on some imaginary planet in a distant galaxy.

Although some standards are being changed to continually ask more of our Littles earlier and earlier, other creative and hands-on activities are being delayed until students are *old enough to comprehend.* Sometimes Littles are limited by the adults around them simply because we often focus on the wrong set of expectations. Littles are not always ready to start reading, writing, or reciting math facts when they're still exploring everything around them. But these are often the primary, or only, targets in traditional schooling. Instead of tackling skills that they're not developmentally ready for, Littles should be creating, building, baking, designing, painting, photographing, composing music, sculpting—the list is endless!

Once, as I took my class of five- to seven-year-olds on a photoshoot to investigate how plants grow, we saw a hawk circling above the tree line. All of a sudden, my students became mini-documentarians! We had iPads with us, and some were taking photos that they would later add to a photo story featuring their own drawings and comments. Some of them switched to video and were narrating everything they could see about that hawk. This opportunity never could have happened if our school had some antiquated policy restricting use of devices until the kids were "old enough" to use them.

Littles are capable of much more than most adults assume. Instead of creating monotony in their day by pushing them toward concepts and skills they aren't developmentally ready to master, why not open up their worlds to exploration and creation? When I provide my students with the tools to create—a paintbrush, an instrument, an iPad or another device— they regularly surprise me with how much they're able to accomplish. I have been truly impressed with the unique perspectives they bring to solving problems and inventing something brand new. I often remind educators that we don't need to teach Littles so much as design an environment where they can flourish and then simply get out of their way.

Michelle Baldwin
(@michelle107)

Lead Teacher at Anastasis Academy,
Denver, Colorado
Avenue4Learning.com

Empowering Littles

Big kids can do cool things with technology—and so can little kids! That was the thought that drove me (Pinto) to explore technology with Littles. My first teaching assignment was with a spring transitional kindergarten class that consisted of four- and five-year-olds. The educational apps and websites that were recommended for this age group were a great place to start, but I knew the students were capable of much more than clicking around, and they needed to create. Because our school had Google for Education accounts, I steered my Littles toward Google Apps for creation. Before I knew it, they were navigating Google Classroom with ease and using various Google Apps to demonstrate the skills they were learning. They constantly amazed me with what they could do. I believe Littles have the potential to do far more than we can imagine. They simply need their teachers to believe in them and to be willing to embrace new and nontraditional learning opportunities.

Our youngest students need to have the opportunity to learn digital literacy and to benefit from a new way of looking at how to learn. Technology opens up new opportunities for students to interact with their learning. Too often, Littles are denied the chance to be part of 1:1 initiatives in schools, and this is a mistake. In kindergarten our students discover what learning looks like. Their world is digital, and they deserve the opportunity to express themselves with tools that will help their voices to be heard. Rather than waiting until third grade to expose students to digital literacy, start with Littles so that when they are older they will have established the basics and can run with the ideas and tools they already know how to use.

Meaningful Tech Integration

The point of using of technology in primary classrooms is not to go paper-less or to abandon manipulatives, blocks, toys, finger paint, read-alouds, and other hands-on experiences that children enjoy. Replacing those activities with computer tasks does not make learning better, and the idea that digital assignments are more engaging than analog activities is a fallacy.

Before deciding to do a digital task, it's helpful to ask, "Why is this better than using paper or manipulatives?" In the primary classroom, kids are learning how to form letters, develop number sense, create sentences, and cut with scissors. Abolishing those foundational skills does not make sense, but digital literacy skills should be *added* to that list. Such skills range from logging into devices to understanding what the red squiggly line under a word means to designing a storyboard.

Technology is available in more classrooms—in more formats—than ever before, and all students (even Littles!) can use it as a learning tool. It's time to make a shift away from simply carving out time to do a technology activity and toward integrating technology into the natural course of a day to enhance overall learning and create new opportunities. Students can use technology to learn more about a topic, practice skills in a new way, collaborate and share their ideas, or even to connect to the outside world, perhaps working with kids in another city or with experts in another state. Meaningful technology integration will take your students beyond the walls of your classroom and give them new ways to be creative and expressive critical thinkers.

The only thing that is constant in life—and teaching—is change. In education, regardless of our titles, our job is to prepare students for the future by pro-viding a wide range of learning opportunities and exposing them to multiple learning tools—technology being one of them.

Oh, the things littles CAN do with technology...

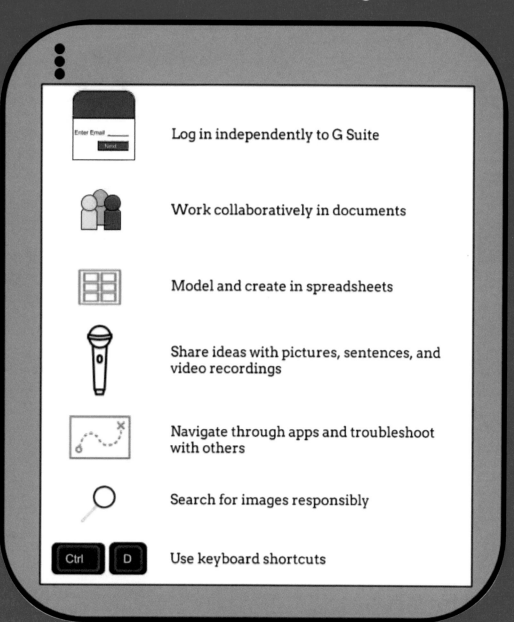

Log in independently to G Suite

Work collaboratively in documents

Model and create in spreadsheets

Share ideas with pictures, sentences, and video recordings

Navigate through apps and troubleshoot with others

Search for images responsibly

Use keyboard shortcuts

Chapter 1
Behind the Scenes

Your school likely already has a G Suite for Education account. Because you picked up this book, our assumption is that you are ready to learn how to use the powerful tools Google provides for teachers to enhance learning and student–teacher interaction: Drive, Classroom, Gmail, Docs, Sheets, Slides, Drawings, Forms, Sites, Hangouts, Calendar, Keep, and Vault.

 Note: If your school is not a G Suite school, it is free to sign up. Each school or district sets up a domain to use with G Suite and appoints a G Suite administrator to manage the accounts. Each teacher and student needs an account created for them on the domain. The G Suite administrator is able to set permissions and restrictions on the apps. You might not have access to some apps, such as Gmail or Hangouts, if the G Suite administrator turned those apps off. Student email also can be restricted by the G Suite administrator to the domain. This means students can only email with other students or adults at the school.

Getting Set Up

The first hurdle you might have to overcome is getting the school to make G Suite accounts for the younger students. Be persistent—your students are capable of using Google Apps and demonstrating learning at high levels. Let us not leave out our youngest learners from using technology. They are the least afraid of trying something new. Helping students become adept at using Google Apps at a young age allows upper-grade teachers to spend more time on activities and curriculum than on basic technology skills.

Email

Teachers do not typically set up student accounts. Someone at the school, usually in the IT department, has administrative access to Google Apps and creates a username and password for each student. The student username is an email address on the school domain. If the school or district is not ready for younger students to have email accounts, this can be disabled by the Google Apps administrator. The login still appears to be an email address, but the students do not have email access.

We recommended that email not be turned off even for the youngest students. Email is an important skill for students to learn, and teachers can use this medium as a platform for assignment creation. For example, students can compose and send the teacher a professional email that includes a recipient, a message, and a signature line to demonstrate their English and language arts skills. Using an email instead of a text document helps students to have a context for their work and fosters digital citizenship and digital literacy skills. The interfaces are different between Gmail and Google Docs; writing an email in Gmail feels more authentic than writing an email in a template in Google Docs. Additionally, Google Apps notifies students of teacher feedback via email. Disabling email from teacher to student can make that feedback process more difficult. Because the school has control of email options and can restrict email to and from younger students to the domain (which means they can only email with people at the school), there is really no need to turn off email capability for any student.

Pinto's Perspective

They CAN Do It!

Why wait until the middle of the school year to give students access to G Suite when they *can* start creating and accessing resources at the beginning of the school year? While the kids may not know all their letter names and be able to identify all their numbers, they *can* match those characters from a login card to the keys on the keyboard.

The Login Process

Teachers don't (or at least shouldn't) assume that older kids are so technologically savvy that they do not need time and assistance logging in to Google Apps the first time. We believe that students as young as four years old are capable of logging in to Google Apps independently. That said, you will need to allow plenty of time for your Littles to log in. Anticipate that the process will be slow the first few times. In education we do not disregard a task or skill when it takes students a while to learn it.

When the kids practice the same task frequently, they get better at it and eventually master it. The same applies with logging in to Google; each time students log in they get better at it.

As with anything, consistency is key. If you are using Google Apps with young students (or even older students), use it a lot. This doesn't mean you need to do several different technology activities with students. Pick three and use them frequently. After you and your students have mastered the skills and classroom management for those three technology tasks, add a new task. The point is to not let the technology get in the way of teaching. No technology improves learning; it's the design of the activity and the lesson planning that make all the difference.

Have the students log in to their devices and then have them log out. Then have them log right back in. Make a challenge out of it! You can create an individualized chart and give the

kids a sticker every time they successfully log in and out. Allowing the students to practice logging in and out of the device is important, even if your students have individual devices.

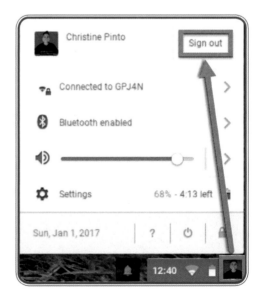

This song, sung to the tune of "Skip to My Lou," can help students remember the sign-out and shutdown process:

Click on your face, and then Sign Out.

Click on your face and then Sign Out.

Click on your face and then Sign Out,

and then it's time to shut it down.

Login Cards

Login cards are essential for Littles, especially when they are given challenging usernames or passwords. These cards, which should include the student's name, login name, and password, can be stored in a pocket chart or student supply boxes, inside of lanyard-style name tag holders, or inside of pencil boxes.

Searching for numbers and letters on the keyboard can take Littles a lot of time. They are just getting familiar with the keyboard and its randomized letters, and some students might still be learning letter and number identification. To prevent letter and number search time from holding back Littles from using technology, you might consider color coding the letters on their login cards. Put colored tape along the left side of the rows of the keyboards to correspond with the background of the letters and numbers on the kids' login cards.

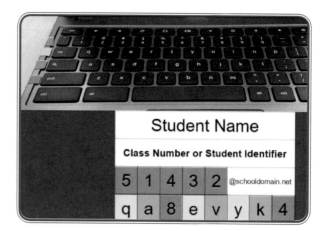

This cuts down on search time, and the students will be less likely to ask you where the letters are on the keyboard. They will understand that "red 2" is in the red row, and they would scan that row for the "2" number key.

Learn More

Editing the Login Card Template:
christinepinto.com/formatlogincard

I have my kindergarteners log in to G Suite on Chromebooks the second day of school.

—Christine Pinto

Profile Pictures

By default, Google Apps uses the first letter of the students' names as their profile pictures. Online interactions are more personal when there is a picture of the student. A profile picture also aids the feedback process because it allows the teacher to more easily identify who is interacting.

One idea for a profile picture is to create cartoon avatars for the students. Cartoon avatar websites and apps creators come and go, so we suggest searching for "cartoon avatar creator" and exploring different options. Look for download options or take a screenshot to capture an image of the avatar. If you are thinking of hav-

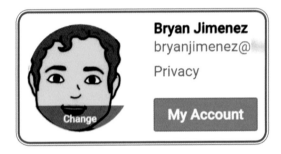

ing your Littles create their own, put yourself in their shoes and look for friendly navigation through the tool and check for inappropriate elements that should be avoided by students.

Alternatively, allow Littles to set their own profile pictures. Students love to take selfies. Allowing them to create their own profile pictures can be a source of pride for students.

Students also can change their profile pictures in Google Classroom. Once in Google Classroom, students click on the menu icon (three lines in the upper left corner). At the bottom, in the *Settings* option, students can update their profile picture. When you're getting your class started with G Suite, consider creating a station where a parent volunteer can help students create and add their Google account avatars.

Learn More		
Nickelodeon Avatar Creator: goo.gl/jfG5FV	**DoppelMe:** doppelme.com	**Cartoonify:** cartoonify.de

Let's Get Started

The best way to learn how to use new resources and technology tools is to explore them. Google Apps are not just applications that the kids use. You can use Google Apps to create resources that will support your instruction, help you collect information from parents and students, and more. If you are new to G Suite and Google Apps, you should go through some tutorials on the basics. Take advantage of the many ready-to-use templates this book offers and then get creative and design your own activities to share with students, families, and colleagues.

Learn More

G Suite Training Center:
gsuite.google.com/learning-center

G Suite Training Chrome
Extension: goo.gl/gNrJY8

Chapter 2
Technology Integration with Littles

It is likely that your students will have interacted with some form of technology before they enter your classroom. Even if they have been using a tablet since they were toddlers, it's not safe to assume that all Littles will know the parts of the device they will be using. To make sure that all students have a good understanding of their devices, hold a class discussion. Start by asking your students what the device is used for. Using words that Littles understand, highlight the parts of the device you'll be referring to most and explain the "job" or function of those parts.

Here's how you might introduce a Chromebook to your Littles:

- **Chromebook**: This is a computer that you use to create things and find out more information.
- **Screen:** This is the part that lets you see what you are doing on the Chromebook.
- **Keyboard**: You use a keyboard to type, just like you use a pencil to write. The keys have letters and numbers, and you push the keys so they appear on the screen.
- **Touchpad or Trackpad**: You slide your finger up and down and around on the trackpad to move your cursor on the screen so you can click on things.

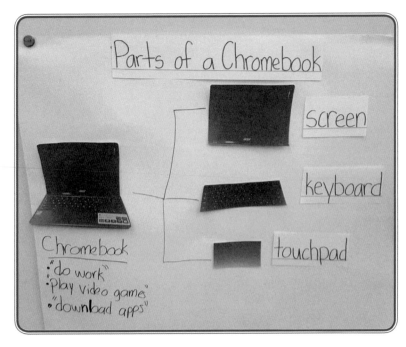

Device Handling and Digital Citizenship

You'll also need to facilitate a conversation with students about how to take care of the device. The kids probably have some ideas, so have them share! Then expand on those ideas.

Establish clear expectations for handling devices. A few rules that should always be included are unplugging devices carefully, holding the device with two hands—particularly while walking—keeping food and drinks away from devices. The kids will want to show you that they can handle the responsibility of taking care of the device. There is also a good chance they will remind each other of proper device care when they see their peers misusing the device.

Discuss digital citizenship. *Digital citizenship* is a term we need to introduce to kids while they are young and beginning to use technology. Being a digital citizen means being responsible, respectful, and mindful when working in a digital environment. Citizenship is often discussed at the beginning of the year. We talk with students about what it entails: being a good friend, setting an example for others, following the rules. Include digital citizenship in that conversation. Continue to discuss digital citizenship throughout the school year, and be sure to praise the class for using technology correctly rather than only bringing attention to digital citizenship when something goes wrong. Some ideas for discussion topics include keeping personal information private, communicating with respect, reporting cyberbullying, and crediting the work of others.

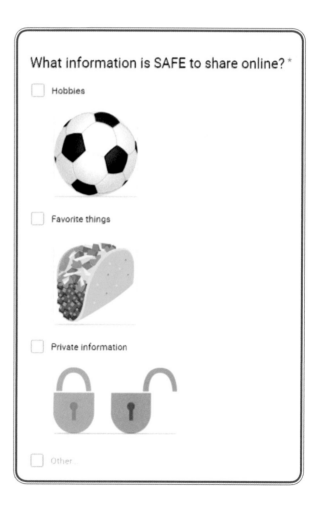

Common Sense Media has an abundance of digital learning resources that can support you in the classroom.

Kids can benefit from comprehensive practice with the concept of digital citizenship. Hans Tullmann, an educational technology coach, created a resource using Google Forms for students to practice demonstrating their understanding of digital citizenship. Students start out reviewing digital citizenship by watching a video from Common Sense Education and then answer some questions about content in the video. At the end, students take the Digital Citizenship Pledge to be safe and practice what they have learned when they are working online.

Learn More

Common Sense Media:
commonsensemedia.org/educators

Template

Digital Citizenship Practice created by Hans Tullmann:
christinepinto.com/tullmanncitizenship

Create a Workflow

Just as you would create a routine for students to line up by the door or pack up at the end of the day, it's also necessary to establish a workflow regarding devices. Think of a traffic flow that you think would work best in your classroom, whether you are 1:1 with devices or have a limited number.

A Chromebook Walk in Pinto's Classroom

Pinto's Perspective

My students complete the "Chromebook walk" when they are going to take their Chromebooks out of the cart. I usually let about five to six kids go to the cart at a time. They know to walk all the way around our tables and wait patiently as only one student gets his or her login card and Chromebook. They carry their Chromebooks with two hands as they walk to sit down. When the kids put their Chromebooks away, they know to plug in the charger and that the number on the Chromebook should face them as they put it back into its own slot inside the cart.

Choose a Seating Arrangement

One way to greatly enhance the integration of technology into your classroom routine is to find an efficient and comfortable seating arrangement. Here are three options that we like:

Center Rotations

Whether your class is 1:1 with devices or has a limited number of devices, you can have your students use those devices through center rotations. If the idea of center rotations is new to you, choose a block of time and divide it into the number of centers you need. For example, if you have a one-hour block, you can have four centers that run for fourteen minutes each with a minute of transition time between each center. If you have parent volunteers or a teacher's aide, station them at one of your centers or have them monitor the kids while they are working in the other centers. Your station will be the technology center, where the kids can work on an activity in the given time. This allows you to work with a small group of kids and be there to coach them and troubleshoot if necessary.

If you are 1:1 with devices, you might eventually want to move away from center rotations because the kids can be working on the same thing at the same time. In the beginning, center rotations are great when the kids are learning how to navigate and use their devices, but you want to be productive with your time. If you keep technology in the center rotations, use it to your advantage. Keep digital activities consistent so that the kids can work on them independently at a center and not need you for technical support. The kids are completely capable of working on their devices independently. This allows you to work with another small group of students or facilitate other centers that require more support.

Learn More

Sample Centers:
christinepinto.com/samplecenters

Gather on the Carpet

The carpet tends to serve as a regular meeting place for students; the kids know it is a place to gather around to learn and share. Students can bring their devices to the carpet area and work on an activity. If your students are 1:1 with devices, the whole class can sit in a big circle with their devices. When the kids are sitting in a circle, this allows them to easily "check out" what

their peers are doing on their devices. The kids are sitting close in proximity and can model on their own screens how to complete an action if their peers need assistance with a task.

Having students gather on the carpet allows you to walk around and monitor and help as necessary. The kids are not sitting for long periods waiting for an answer on how to do something, because another peer close by can help them. And remember, it is okay if children need to spend a little time solving a problem. Let them persevere! The goal with learning is to help students learn to troubleshoot and solve problems.

Arrange Workspaces for Collaboration

Some teachers are more comfortable having their students work in designated workstations in the classroom. This classroom layout option puts students in small groups so they can work collaboratively.

Whatever device situation you're working with in your classroom, remember that you don't have to tackle technology integration alone. Embrace any help that's offered, and get parent volunteers or technology coaches involved. Have a plan, and have others help you carry out that plan. Consider buddying up your class with a class from an older grade level to work on activities together. When you connect your Littles to older students, they have their own personal coaches.

Google Apps for Multiple Devices

G Suite for Education works on almost any device. Students can locate their assignments on a Chromebook, iPad, or PC. Before you introduce G Suite to your Littles, it's helpful to consider device setup and organization to create a productive workflow. Whether all of your students have their own device to use or you only have devices for half the class or you share devices with the entire grade level, it's important that you assign students to the device they will regularly use. This works to foster a sense of responsibility among students and also helps with device management. Another tip is to make the Google Apps easily accessible for students. The setup phase will look a little different depending on the device students are using.

Chromebook Users

When students log in to their Chromebooks, they are automatically logged in to their G Suite accounts. The Chrome browser icon is found toward the bottom of the desktop view in what is called *the shelf.* Some app shortcuts such as Gmail, Docs, or YouTube might be saved in the shelf. Students can access Google Apps by clicking on the *Launch* icon in the shelf or by clicking on the *Search* key on the keyboard. Add the Google Classroom app to Chromebooks from the Chrome webstore (goo.gl/31NFPI).

To keep track of which students are using which Chromebook, consider putting some form of identifier—a number, sticker, or mark—on the device so students are able to easily identify their device when the time comes. If you have access to a cart, it's also a good idea to label device slots and charging cords with the same identifier so students can independently plug in their devices correctly.

PC Users

To access G Suite from a desktop or laptop, a student will use the Chrome browser. If possible, Google Classroom should be set as the default homepage for students. If students are going to be using Chrome extensions, additional digital tools powered by Chrome, have your students sign in to Chrome. By signing in to Chrome, students will be able to save bookmarks, use extensions, and customize their toolbar. Signing out of devices is an essential habit for students to acquire. If you're sharing

devices or a computer lab, it becomes even more important that students sign out when they are finished. Chrome remembers users who are logged in. On clicking on the Chrome browser, the student's account will load and be accessible, unless the student signs out of his or her account. When students sign out, Chrome remembers their Google address, which is helpful for Littles because then they only have to enter their password to sign in.

If you are working with small groups or a half-class set of desktops or laptops, the setup will be similar to that for Chromebooks. Use a device identifier and assign students to the specific device they will use regularly. If you're working in a computer lab, assign students to a specific computer, and develop a seating chart to help them remember where to sit.

Learn More

Add a Chrome User Tutorial:
christinepinto.com/addchromeuser

iPad or Tablet Users

On an iPad or tablet, students will need the G Suite apps installed. Put all of the G Suite apps in a single folder on the device. We suggest putting the folder in the taskbar or on the homepage. Note that some features in Google Apps that are present on a computer are not available on a tablet.

Group Apps and Put in Taskbar

Find a place on the tablet to put a device identifier for Littles to easily recognize. We like putting students' names on the back of the devices so that if they forget which device they use, it can be found quickly.

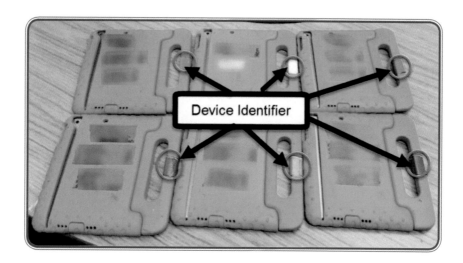

Generally, when users are signed in to a tablet, they stay signed in until they are removed. This is somewhat of a double-edged sword. For Littles, switching accounts on a tablet is easy and fast; however, they potentially have access to other students' accounts and work. They might not intend to access someone else's account, but it is easy to work in someone else's account and not realize it.

There are two options to prevent students from accessing their classmates' accounts:

1. **Leave students signed in.** If you choose this option, your students should develop the habit of tapping on the three-line menu, tapping the small arrow, and selecting their account to ensure that they aren't working in another student's account. If the tablets are stored in your classroom and not being shared with another class, this option might be best for your students.

2. **Have students remove themselves every time they are finished working with the device.**

For example, on an iPad, students would repeat the same navigation pattern as option one, with the additional steps of clicking on *Manage accounts* and tapping on *Remove.* This means they would have to retype their login information the next time they use the device. If you are sharing tablets with other classes, option two might make the most sense.

When I (Pinto) was working with the four- and five-year-olds, I shared six iPads with two other Google Apps–using classes. They were capable of taking on the responsibility of switching accounts (option one). It was part of the workflow; the kids knew it was an essential piece of accessing their work. You know your students well, and you can decide which option is best.

Chapter 3
Explore Google Classroom

Google Classroom is hands-down the easiest way to facilitate blended learning. It provides a space where you can seamlessly distribute digital activities, share online resources, provide collaboration opportunities among students, and even open avenues for providing feedback to students. (You'll learn more about each of these features in the chapters that follow.)

Before Google Classroom, the sharing of Google Documents with students could be a bit of a chore. Google Classroom makes it easy to add any document from Google Drive into an assignment. Classroom takes care of the sharing permissions automatically, thus avoiding students frustrated that they cannot access a document. Classroom allows you to go beyond simply allowing students to view your documents. Notice the tiny triangle next to the *Students can view file* option. The middle option, *Students can edit file*, allows students to collaborate on the same document. The third option, *Make a copy for each student,* instantly generates a copy per student and adds the student's name to the document title.

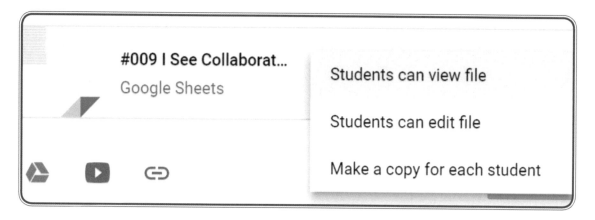

Google Classroom allows teachers to be more productive with their time to design lessons and have meaningful interactions with kids. Use Google Classroom as a hub that provides links to templates and documents from Google Drive, which makes accessing student work and keeping track of their progress possible.

Google Classroom is the starting point for all Google Apps activities, but it is not limited to only Google Apps. We have our students always start out in Google Classroom, regardless of the digital tool they will be using during assignments. This is why we recommended having Google Classroom as the starting point

Keeler's Tips

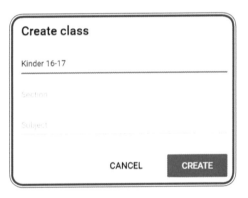

Be on the hunt for the tiny triangle. You will see these all over Google Apps in G Suite. The tiny triangle indicates more choices—CLICK ON IT!

for all online activities and even some nondigital activities. If possible, set Google Classroom as the students' homepage when they log in to Chrome on the Chromebook. On a PC or tablet, make sure the Classroom app icon is easy to access.

Establish a routine in which students obtain their device, log in, and go to Google Classroom. They will quickly pick up on the navigation pattern in Google Classroom to find assignments. Here are three suggestions that can improve the workflow with your Littles:

Choose a Simple Class Title

When you create a Google Classroom, think of a short title for the name of your class so students can easily locate it.

Create class

Kinder 16-17

Section

Subject

CANCEL   CREATE

Title Assignments with a Hashtag and Number

Use a hashtag with a three-digit number in the title of all assignments. The hashtag, such as #001, #002, or #003, will distinguish an assignment from other numbers. Write the assignment number in big print on the board for students to match in Google Classroom. Your students may not be able to read assignment titles, but they can identify a symbol (the hashtag) and a number. From the technical standpoint, titling your activities with a hashtag and number can help you out when searching for those items in Google Drive. In Drive, a folder for Google Classroom is auto-matically created, and as you create your assignments a folder is made that gives you access to student Docs. The hashtag and number system helps to keep those folders and Docs organized in Google Drive.

Christine Pinto
Nov 23, 2016

Word Families

#014 Inserting -at Images
Click on OPEN
Click on CREATE - select Slides.
Click on IMAGE (mountain picture) to insert an image. Click on Search. Type an -at word.
Click on the T text box icon to insert a text box. Type the -at word that matches your image

Put Frequently Used Sites in the About Tab

The About tab in Google Classroom can be a place for sites or games that students will access regularly. Instead of having the kids bookmark commonly used pages, put the links in the About tab. A thumbnail-sized image appears next to the site, and kids can identify the site or source based on the image.

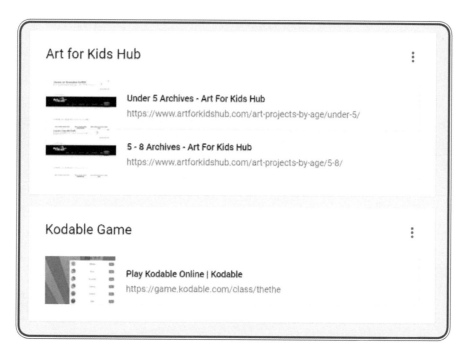

Art for Kids Hub

Under 5 Archives - Art For Kids Hub
https://www.artforkidshub.com/art-projects-by-age/under-5/

5 - 8 Archives - Art For Kids Hub
https://www.artforkidshub.com/art-projects-by-age/5-8/

Kodable Game

Play Kodable Online | Kodable
https://game.kodable.com/class/thethe

Add Topics

When creating an assignment in Google Classroom, you can add a topic. This allows the student to filter the assignments in the Stream. Rather than using the categories we traditionally use in the gradebook, consider how the students would want to filter the assignments. Some teachers choose to create a Google Classroom per subject, others prefer to use one Google Classroom and use the topics to filter by subject.

Pinto's Perspective

I am one of those teachers who prefers to have one Google Classroom and apply topics that I think make sense to my students. Some of those include:

- Exploring
- Buddies (activities with older students)
- Alphabet
- Sight Words
- Shapes
- Addition
- Which One Doesn't Belong?
- Writing
- Learning Games
- Extended Challenges

Keeler's Tips

Homework can be a source of stress and fighting for some families. Instead of sending home paperwork, which research shows to have no benefit in primary grades, provide families with conversations that will positively benefit the child's learning and confidence about school.

Learn More

Tour of Google Classroom: 50thingsbook.com

Parent Corner

Consider creating a Parent Corner in the description of each Google Classroom assignment. Typically when we write directions the audience is the student, which can leave parents wondering about what is going on. Rather than the parent needing to contact you for clarification, include a note directly written for an audience of parents. Also include specific reflection questions, which do not require an answer key, that parents can ask their child about the activity. Reflection is shown to have important benefits for learning. Including specific reflection questions ensures that parents can participate in their child's education in a meaningful way.

Which One Doesn't Belong

Due Aug 24

#006 Day 2 Which One Doesn't Belong?

Take a look at the different shapes. Which shape do you think doesn't belong? Think of one reason why that shape does not belong and share it with your elbow partner.

Parent Corner
Parents, we have been studying shapes and their attributes. Your child should be able to choose one shape that doesn't belong, and explain why based on the attributes of the shape (size, color, number of sides/corners, type of shape).

Reflection Question: What is something you know about each of the shapes?

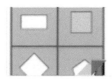

WODB 2.png

Image

Nondigital

Not everything that happens in class is digital; in fact, a lot is not! Adding nondigital activities to Google Classroom has many benefits. Adults who are working with Littles can benefit from knowing what nondigital activities the child is involved in as well. Consider using the Google Classroom Stream to reflect the activities of the day. Include a Parent Corner for nondigital assignments with an explanation of the learning goals along with the reflection questions.

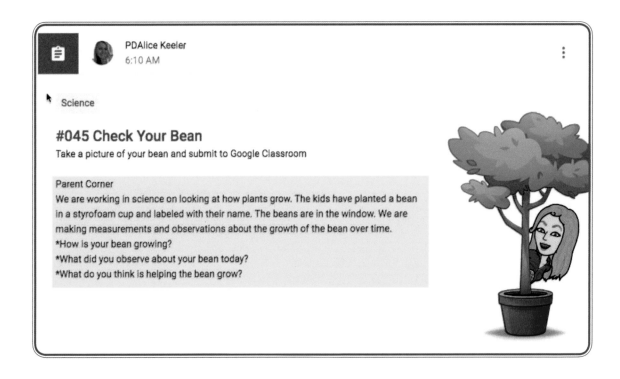

Private Comments for Observations

Each assignment provides a space to leave Private Comments for students. While students are engaged in nondigital activities, consider leaving notes and observations in the Private Comments. The Private Comments area provides a place to record information about students' skills and behaviors and is easily accessible for the teacher and students.

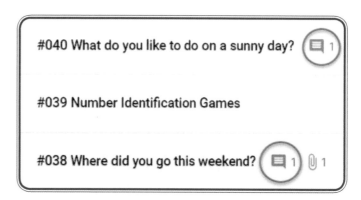

The Google Classroom mobile app makes it easy to record student observations. Open the app and locate the nondigital activity in the Google Classroom Stream. Swipe over to *Student Work* to view a roster. Tap on any student name to reveal the option to *Add private comment* for that student. Parents, when sitting with their child reviewing Google Classroom together, can click on the *About* tab to select *Your work*. This provides a list of Google Classroom work and the assignment status. On any assignment with a comment, a comment icon appears.

After completing nondigital work, the student can use the blue *Mark as done* button, or you can use the *Returned* button to notate that the work has been completed. This prevents the student and parent from seeing multiple assignments with the status of *Assigned*.

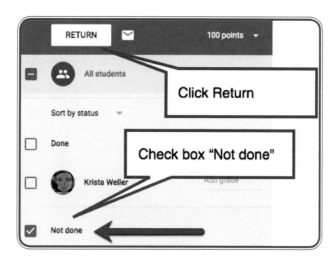

Sample Assignments

  Christine Pinto
Nov 2

Writing

#035 What weather do you like?

AT SCHOOL: Kiddos, use the weather thinking map to help you answer today's prompt: What weather do you like? Write a complete sentence and draw a picture to go with your sentence.

AT HOME (Parent Corner):
-What weather type did you choose?
-Why do you like this type of weather?
-What type of weather is your LEAST favorite?

 **Thinking Maps 2017-2018**
Google Slides

Graphing

#032 Halloween Scene

AT SCHOOL: Kiddos, double click on the haunted house, and add ghosts, pumpkins and bats to your Halloween Scene.
Graph the amount of each item you used by typing anything into the cells in the graph.
Complete the sentences by typing the numbers of each item you used.

AT HOME (Parent Corner): The kids are working on identifying numbers and practicing one-to-one correspondence by counting.
Which item had the most?
Which item had the least?
How did you know which item had the most and which item had the least?

Leader in Me focus

#026 What does a good citizen do? (Part 2)

AT SCHOOL: We read the story "What if Everybody Did That" and thought about the not so good things the boy did and what he could do INSTEAD. We added more to our 'good citizen' thinking map. One of the focuses for habit 2 (Begin with the End in Mind) is to look for ways to be a good citizen.

AT HOME (Parent Corner):
You may choose to listen to the story with your child (see first link..start video at 18 seconds).
Ask your child:
What are some ways to be a good citizen at home?
What are some ways to be a good citizen when we are out and about at the store, church, etc?
Please leave your child's comments in the private comments section.

What if Everybody Did That (Read Aloud)
YouTube video   3 minutes

Thinking Maps 2017-2018
Google Slides

Non-Google Classroom Users

If you are not a Google Classroom user, you will need to use a different digital tool to distribute Google Apps to students. Consider using Doctopus, which is an add-on that allows you to set access levels for templates that can be for your whole class or for individual students.

Learn More

Doctopus:
cloudlab.newvisions.org/add-ons/doctopus

Chapter 4
Activities Littles Can Do

Your Littles can do so much with technology, even if they have never used a device before coming to school. In this chapter, we'll share ideas about activities you can use with your students. You are the facilitator of learning in your classroom, and you know your students' needs and academic goals. Modify these beginner-friendly templates to benefit your students.

As you explore the activities below, remember that children (like adults) need opportunities to explore new digital tools. You might get them started by showing them some basics and what to click on; however, if you show kids five things they will only do those five things. Sometimes people struggle with technology because they are afraid to click on things. We do not want our kids to have to ask for permission to click on something or be afraid. Encourage them to explore and *ask* the kids what the icons do instead of telling them what they do. Digital literacy starts with icon identification and understanding what actions can be completed by clicking on the icons. Icons are the same across the Google Apps, and many of those icons are universal with other apps and platforms; for example, if students see a pencil icon, they should know that it would typically mean to edit something. Let them explore, click, and learn!

Create Drawings

Although not available on tablets, using Google Drawing on a Chromebook is a great way to get students started with using Google Apps. Tablet users can create drawings and explore toolbars on non–G Suite apps; there are many to choose from. Google Slides is a wonderful alternative to Google Drawing. It uses the same drawing engine as Google Drawing and works on a tablet. Using Google Classroom, students can create blank drawing documents easily and get started with using Google Drawing.

Learn More

Click on Create Video:

christinepinto.com/clickoncreate

#002 Exploring Google Drawing

Click OPEN, then the CREATE button and select Drawings.
Watch the video to review these steps
Click on the icons to add items to your Drawing.

Parent Corner
This is one of the kids' first activities where they are exploring
in Google Apps. They are developing the foundational skills to
digital literacy by discovering what icons do.
Reflection Questions: What did you learn to add to your
Drawing? What did you click on to add those things?

 **Click on CREATE.mp4**
Video

Word Collage

In Google Drawing, students can create a word collage with adjectives that describe themselves and accompany their collage with a selfie. When using the Alice Keeler Webcam Screenshot extension, students can take a snapshot with their webcam. The image is automatically saved in a folder in the student's Drive. The student can insert the image from Drive, or paste the link to the image, which is copied to the clipboard. Additionally, students can use the *Insert* menu and add some Word Art and type words that describe themselves and place them around their selfie.

Learn More

Alice Keeler Webcam Screenshot:
alicekeeler.com/webcamscreenshot

Upgrade to Google Slides

What students can do in Google Drawing translates almost exactly to Google Slides for most things. Google Slides has the added advantage of multiple pages. Unlike Google Drawing, you can lock down template elements to the background in Google Slides by using the Slide Master. This helps students move and manipulate shapes without the graphic organizer elements getting in the way.

In Google Slides, Littles can insert shapes to demonstrate their understanding of a concept, whether it be for arrays, math equations, attribute identification, or representing a number. Students click on the shapes icon, select a shape, and place it onto a Slide. Students can change the color of the shapes by clicking on the shape to select it (it will be outlined in blue) and then clicking on the paint bucket and choosing a color. Have students repeat the pattern of inserting a shape until they have the correct amount of shapes to correspond with the number on the slide.

> ## Template
>
> **Numbers 1–10 on Slides:**
> christinepinto.com/numberslides
>
> **Numbers 1–20 with Ten Frames on Slides:**
> christinepinto.com/tenframeslides

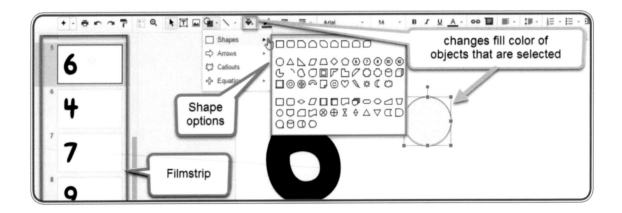

The "Numbers 1–10 on Slides" template contains layouts with numbers on the Slides. The Slides can be moved around within the filmstrip so your students can practice identifying the numbers out of order. Slides also can be deleted if you want your students to practice only a given set of numbers.

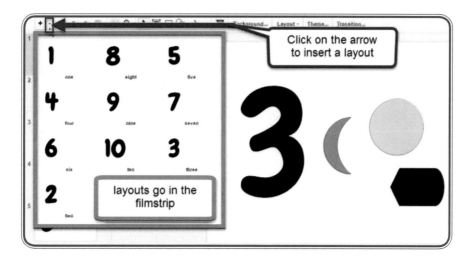

Learn More

Slide Master Tutorial: christinepinto.com/slidemastertutorial

Make Arrangements

Students can step up to the challenge of creating different arrangements of the shapes they inserted and recording their results. When they are finished, students can partner up to compare their work and share observations and strategies. An important element of mathematics is understanding that it is about patterns.

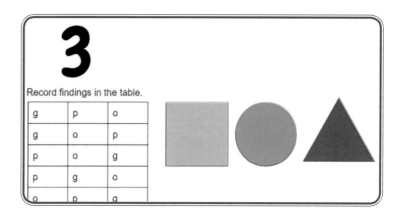

Template

Arrangements template: christinepinto.com/arrange

Voice Typing

Primary students of all levels are learning to read by identifying high-frequency words, word families, and other words with patterns. As with any voice-to-text tool, sometimes what is being spoken is not dictated correctly, and Littles can identify whether words match.

Template

Read Your Sight Words:
alicekeeler.com/readsightwords

In the "Read Your Sight Words" template, students read aloud the sight words in the box and determine whether their spoken words match the words in the box. The kids can select letters or words that are not matching and change the font color to red. With this activity, students are becoming aware of concepts of print. By observing the accuracy of the dictation, the kids will notice whether words start with capitals and understand how many words there are by the spacing between each word.

The voice typing feature is located in the *Tools* menu of Google Docs. After selecting *Voice typing*, a microphone will appear on the screen on the side of the doc. Have students place the cursor in the box below the sight words and read the sight words.

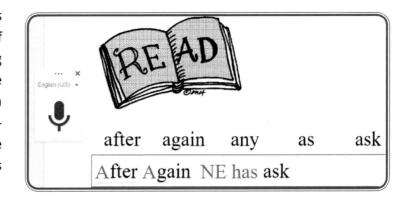

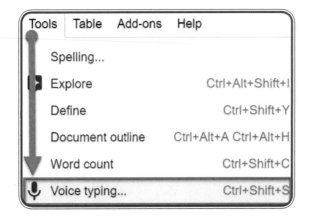

Another activity to try with voice typing is to have children tell their stories. Littles have wonderful ideas and thoughts that can sometimes be formulating faster than they can write or type. Allow students to voice record their stories or assignments so that they come up as text in Google Docs. Afterwards, the kids can edit the text and apply critical thinking skills to fix any errors.

You can also allow students to use voice typing for their response to questions. In the "Voice Type Responses" template, type in questions for your students. The kids can voice record their answer by clicking in the box under the question, accessing the *Tools* menu, and selecting *Voice typing*.

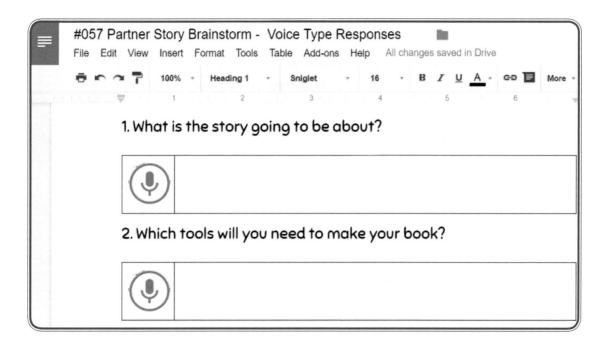

Template

Voice Typing Responses: alicekeeler.com/voicetyperesponses

Pixel Art

Littles can explore and create in Google Sheets spreadsheets. Use the "Pixel Art Spreadsheet" template to get started. The spreadsheet is formatted so that individual cells change color based on a single digit that is typed in the cells. Students are, in effect, painting by number. They become familiar with maneuvering in Google Sheets by pressing the enter key to move to the cell underneath or using the arrow keys to move to different cells. Let the kids explore rather than telling them how to make pictures. Limit your instructions to, "Type a number to see the square cell change color."

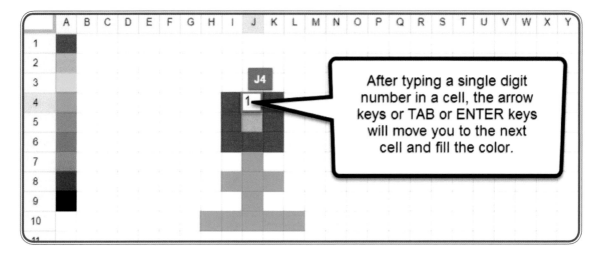

After typing a single digit number in a cell, the arrow keys or TAB or ENTER keys will move you to the next cell and fill the color.

While creating pixel art, students can practice their number identification skills by corresponding a number with a color. They need to think along the lines of, "If I want red in the cell, I need to type the number 1." However, first and second graders can take pixel art in a different direction to practice addition and subtraction fluency.

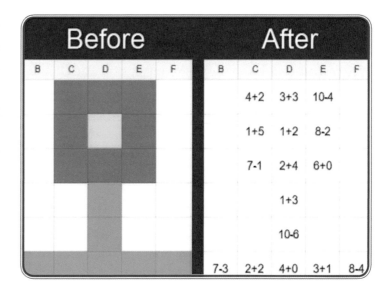

First, they create a picture just as they would in the "Pixel Art" template. Next, they duplicate the sheet so they have an answer sheet. Students can make their image disappear by clicking on the cell with the color and creating an equation to correspond with the cell's number as a sum or a difference. For example, if the cell is purple and has the value of 6, the equations the student can type include 3+3, 5+1, 7-1, or 4+2.

The real fun comes in when the kids share their hidden picture with friends so they can solve the problems and discover the hidden picture. Encourage students to duplicate the equations sheet so they have a master copy of the equations.

To share the spreadsheet, students just click on the blue *Share* button, enter the email address of the person with whom they want to share the activity, and write a message. By default, the student on the receiving end will have editing access.

If email is one of the Google Apps that your district allows students to access, then the receiving student will get an email notifying them that a document was shared with them. The student can also locate the document in their Google Drive. Once in

Google Drive, the receiving student will click on *Shared with me*. The student will then find the shared document. The student can click on the document, single click on a cell with the equation, and type in the sum or difference on top. The equation will go away and the cell color will fill. The student will discover the hidden picture.

Template

Pixel Art:
alicekeeler.com/pixelart

Hidden Image Tutorial:
christinepinto.com/hiddenimagetutorial

Hidden Picture:
alicekeeler.com/hiddenpicture

Sample Hidden Pixel Art Image:
christinepinto.com/hiddenimage

Count ones, tens, hundreds template:
alicekeeler.com/hundredspixel

Write Their Names

Kids love to be creative. Look for ways they can add their own personal touch to any assignment. An easy assignment to use to get started with G Suite and Google Classroom is to ask students to create a Google Document and put their name on it. Encourage your Littles to use their imaginations. They will discover they can easily change the font, font size, and color. It only takes one student to giggle and show a neighbor how their name is huge and pink before all the kids start having fun with it.

Christine Pinto
7:15 AM

Independent Activity

#002 Type Your Name
Click on OPEN.
Click on the CREATE button.
Create a Google Google Doc (Blue).
Click on the document that is created.
Be creative!
Click on TURN IN.

#002 Type Your Name DIRECTIONS
Google Docs

No template is necessary. In Google Classroom students can create a blank Google Doc and have it linked right in Classroom. Show students the *Create* button and how to choose the blue icon to open their Google Doc.

Even if your students can't read directions yet, write them down anyway, with the understanding that a parent or other adult might be reading the directions to assist the child. Creating a Google text document with screenshots of the steps can help nonreaders be independent when using technology. Screenshots, images, and animated GIFs can be dragged right onto the Google Doc. Create a sequence of screenshots to show what to do.

There are many ways to take screenshots, including a variety of Chrome extensions. The screenshot tool Snagit works on PCs and Macs. Annotating the screenshot allows you to draw arrows on the screenshot to help the child see where to click. Additionally, you can record short videos and easily save them as an animated GIF. A GIF is an image that will loop like a movie, right in a Google Doc. Drag the GIF from Snagit right onto the Google Doc.

Template

Sample Directions Document: alicekeeler.com/typeyourname

Learn More

Educator Pricing for Snagit:
christinepinto.com/snagitedu

SlideShot Extension:
alicekeeler.com/slideshot

QuickShare Screenshot:
alicekeeler.com/quickshare

Screencastify screen recording tool
(discounted link for premium account):
screencastify.com/gafe4littles

Check Their Spelling

One way that using technology can be an improvement compared with paper is the ability for the students to have immediate feedback. Using a spreadsheet, conditional formatting can be used to check student answers. For a cell or range of cells, use the *Format* menu and choose *Conditional formatting*. In the side panel, select the criteria for which the cells will format. One option is *Text is exactly*. When the value of the cell is exactly the criteria you selected, the cell will format a color of your choosing to indicate feedback.

In this "Spelling Practice" template, students type their spelling words into the cells. Conditional formatting checks the words against the spelling or vocabulary words in the Spelling List tab. You might want to hide the sheet. Click on the tiny triangle on the Spelling List tab and choose *Hide sheet*. After replacing the default words, distribute a copy to each student to practice.

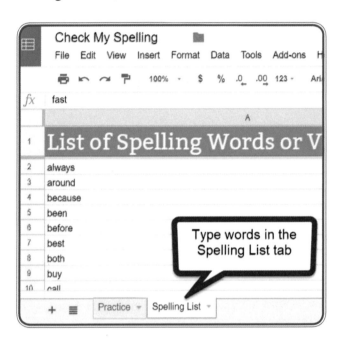

Template

Spelling Practice Template:
alicekeeler.com/checkmyspelling

Kyle's Spelling Practice:
tinyurl.com/kylespelling

Master Control-Z

A common concern many technology users have is "messing up." One of the amazing things about Littles is their lack of fear when it comes to clicking. We do not want to discourage students from being curious, so let them explore! Exploring the apps and trying new things allows students to stretch their abilities, and they even teach you something new in the process. This freedom empowers them not to be afraid of technology. It is culturally acceptable in the twenty-first century not to be an expert at everything, so enjoy exploring some new things with your students. Your students' best day is when they get to teach you something, so ask them to and celebrate what they discover.

It does not take long for Littles to be masters of the undo. Note that many applications have some form of an undo button, like an icon of an arrow going back. Knowing the keyboard shortcut for *undo* can be a lifesaver. After doing something, use *Control-Z* to undo it.

An activity that Littles can do to help them learn *Control-Z* is to have them place objects on Google Slides. For example, students can place an image of a baseball on a slide. They move the ball a little and repeat this task until it has moved all the way across the slide. Then they will show you their animation by using *Control-Z* multiple times. The trick is that the animation will be backwards. Help students to think about planning their story or animation in reverse.

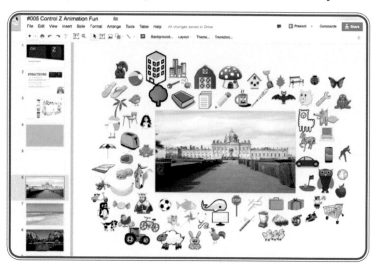

Template

Control Z Story Template: alicekeeler.com/controlzstory

Restore a File

The *Version history* tool in Google Apps allows you to view the document as it looked at a previous point in time, and restore it. When your students' work gets messed up, they can use the *File* menu and choose *Version history*. The sidebar menu shows timestamps of when the file was edited. Click on the timestamps in the sidebar to view the document as it looked at that time. If the document was messed up, find a revision in the sidebar that is correct. Click on *Restore this version* to put it back the way it was.

Search Images with Word Families

Even the youngest Littles are entirely capable of typing words and searching for images. Apply the basic language skills the kids are learning by using various word and phonics patterns (words have some type of spelling pattern to them). For example, with the "at" word family, students know they only need substitute the first letter of the word to create a new word: hat, bat, cat, rat, etc. They can use the image icon (mountain picture) and search these words within the Google Apps.

For this activity, you do not need to give the kids a template because they are inserting their own images and can add text boxes. Indicate in the Google Classroom directions that the student will click on the *CREATE* button to add a Google Slides presentation.

While working in Google Slides, students can use the default title slide to give their project a title and type their name. Text placeholders on the slide layouts make it easy for students to add text. Students can add additional slides multiple ways. Using a Chromebook or computer, students can select the slide tile on the left-hand side and press enter. They can also use the plus icon in the toolbar to add an additional slide. Tablet users will use the plus icon in the bottom right to add additional slides.

Word Families

Due Oct 6, 2017

#014 Inserting -at Images
Click OPEN, then CREATE and select Slides.
Insert text boxes and pictures of -at words.
Watch the video to review how to complete these steps.

Parent Corner:
Parents, the kids are beginning to apply what they know of letter sounds to spelling words.
What do all of these words have in common? (They rhyme! They have the same middle and end sounds/letters).
What makes each word different? (The beginning sound/letter.)

   **at images activity directions.mp4**
Video

The *Explore* button is a button that can be found on the bottom right of the screen when working on computer or Chromebook platforms. It will suggest graphical layouts based on the content on the slide. The kids can select a design they like. Adding images to a slide is a snap when using the image icon in the toolbar. Students search for and add the images to their slide.

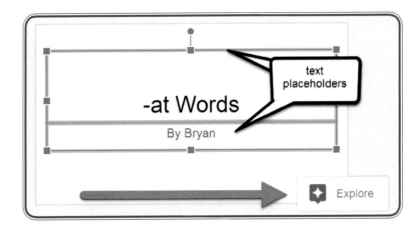

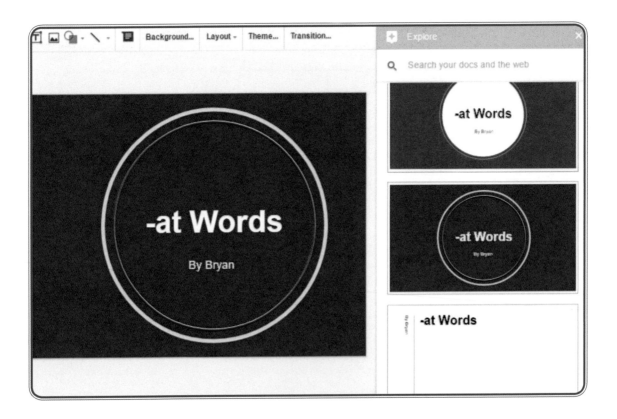

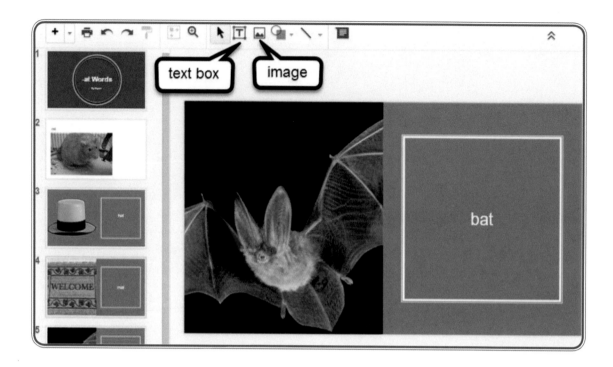

Create All About Me Slides

Kids *want* to share about themselves. In fact, they need to be given opportunities to express themselves and share their voices. The "All About Me" activity is the perfect fit for Littles. The idea is that students take pictures of themselves and their learning environment to share about who they are and what they have learned. Alternatively, this activity can be modified so students can share about themselves at the beginning of the year with their peers. They can insert a sentence of text to describe what is being portrayed in the image.

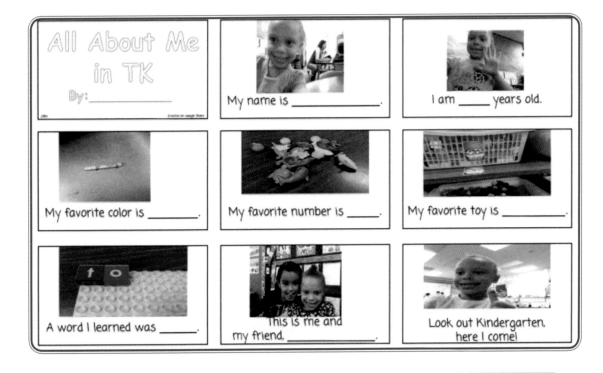

Pinto's Perspective

You can customize this "All About Me" template to fit your students' abilities and academic focuses. I designed this template for my transitional kindergarten students. (The sentence frames were part of the Slides layouts.) My students completed this project over the course of a few days, inserting all of their pictures and resizing them. We used whatever technology we had access to, and they took some of their pictures on the iPads and some on Chromebooks. When the project was complete, I printed out the Slides, two on a page, to create a book for each student. Because writing is a big skill for transitional kindergarteners, they wrote their responses on top of the lines.

Template

All About Me Slides: christinepinto.com/allaboutmeslides

Scavenger Hunts

Students acquire a lot of vocabulary and academic language throughout the school year. A fun way for kids to identify with the vocabulary is for them to go on a scavenger hunt around the classroom or school in search of different words.

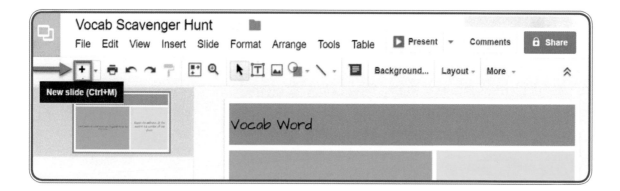

In this Google Slides "Vocabulary Scavenger Hunt" template, students take a picture of the vocabulary term they see and place it over the green box, type the term in the blue box at the top, and type a description in the yellow box to demonstrate their understanding of that term. From a tablet, Littles can use the voice-to-text feature to describe their images. Touchscreen Chromebooks, such as the Acer R11, provide the option to voice type when using the on-screen keyboard. It does not need to be 100 percent free of grammatical or spelling errors. The idea is to connect to terms that they are learning about. When finished, they can click on the + icon in the app to add another slide.

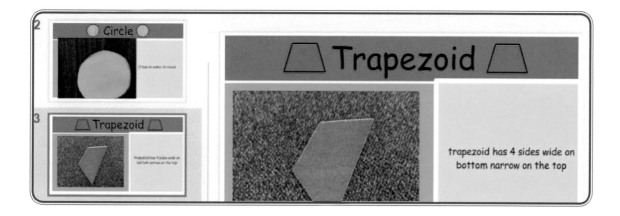

For Chromebook classrooms, having at least one donated mobile phone or tablet for the class can aid in adding pictures to Google Slides. The same Google Slides presentation can be edited on different devices at the same time. Students can be working on the slides on their Chromebook while also having the same Slides presentation open on a mobile device. Any images added to the Slides from the mobile device automatically appear on the presentation on the Chromebook. The ability to work on a project simultaneously from multiple devices is an advantage of using Google Apps.

The Google Drive app on a mobile device allows you to take pictures directly into a shared folder. Share a folder with the students and allow the students to use the Google Drive app to upload pictures into that folder. When working on their Chromebook or PC, the students can insert the pictures from the shared folder by using the *Insert* menu, choosing *Image*, and selecting *Google Drive*. We suggest using the same shared folder for pictures all year.

Template

Vocab Scavenger Hunt: alicekeeler.com/vocabscavengerhunt

Chapter 5
Collaborative Awesomeness

Collaboration is a super-skill in twenty-first-century learning. Working collaboratively in Google Apps means kids are in the same Google document and are working *at the same time*. That means kids of all ages need to understand how to share digital space and collaborate with their peers. Acquiring these skills takes some practice and perseverance—for students and teachers. But it can be done!

Just as we take time to help students know how to be respectful and follow rules in the library, we need to help students understand how to work on a shared document. Expect that the first couple of times students collaborate on a document there might be some disarray and some tears. It can be difficult for students to be aware of their surroundings physically and just as difficult for them to be aware of others around them digitally. Have digital citizenship conversations with students to have them explain how they know where someone else is typing.

Here are a few of our favorite collaborative activities:

Collaborative Slides

When working in the same Google Slides, you will be able to see other collaborators who are in the slides at the same time. Their first initial or profile picture will appear at the top of the document. You can tell *where* someone is editing because their work area will be highlighted or indicated in some way.

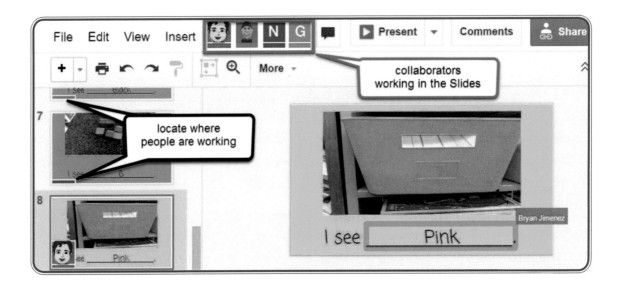

One tip is to remind students, "Slides are free—make a new one." If a student is inadvertently typing on another student's slide, the best strategy is to just abandon the slide and make a new one. It can be frustrating to have your slide taken over by someone else; usually this is a result of the other student just not paying attention to where they are working.

The first time you do anything new with students, they will want to push buttons and see what they can do. This likely may include unintentional or even intentional deleting or altering the work of other students. Plan for this to happen. Your first collaborative slides activities should be something not graded, yet academic. When student work is lost, although it is upsetting to the student, it won't be a big deal. Have students talk about how to be polite and respectful to others while collaborating online; allow the students to develop norms for synchronous collaboration.

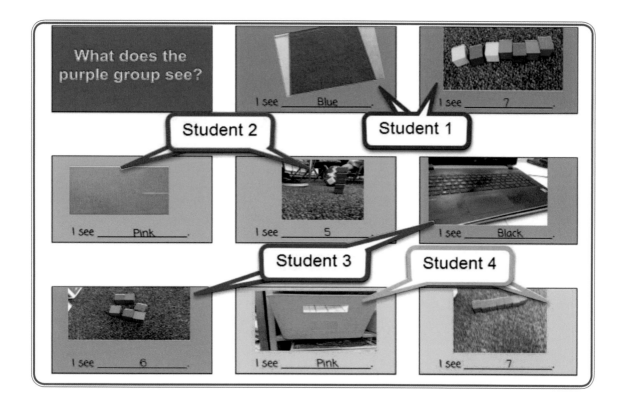

Collaborative work can start out in small groups. For example, have four students working together on the same Google Slides rather than everyone in the class working on the same document. In Google Slides, you can design a template with colored slides, and students each can be assigned a color. They can work on the slide that is their color. To accommodate for students who are colorblind, add a small clip art image in the corner of each colored slide; for example, put a tiger on the orange slide, a flower on the green slide, and a snail on the blue slide.

Four- and five-year-olds have worked together in the "I See Collaborative Slides" template. In the activity, the kids went around the classroom with tablets and took pictures of colors they saw or quantities that they could count.

From the "I See Collaborative Slides" template, students have the option of adding a slide with a layout with different colors.

1. Students locate the layout that matches their assigned color.

2. They insert an image from the camera (on a tablet) or by using the Webcam Screenshot extension on a computer or Chromebook platform.

3. They crop the image and center it on the slide.

4. They click on the text placeholder and type either a color or a number of something they saw in the classroom.

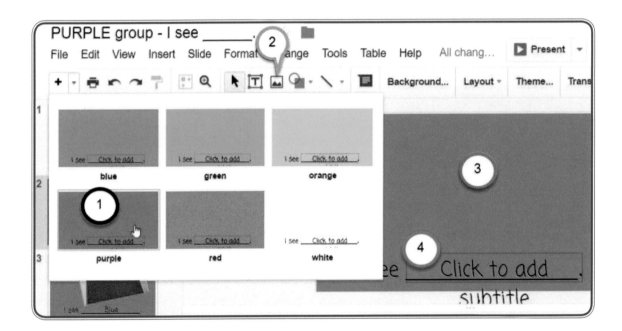

Template

I See Collaborative Slides (small group):
christinepinto.com/iseecollaborativeslides

On the Hunt for Syllables:
christinepinto.com/syllablehunt

Whole Class Collaborative Slides:
alicekeeler.com/groupslides

Assigning Collaborative Docs to Groups

Create a Google Slides template with a graphic organizer for the slide layouts and make a copy of this template for each small group. Edit the document titles to include the students' names; for example, "Toya Bonham, Earnest Deppen, Houston Lococo, Orval Gaines #059 On the Hunt for Syllables." To be more efficient with your time, you can use the "Copy Docs Classes" template, which can assist with creating the copies and renaming the documents. Type the names of the students that you want in the group in column A of the Names tab in the spreadsheet. Click on the *Create copies* in the menu and choose a document that you would like to have copies of. After authorizing permission for the spreadsheet to run, an additional tab will appear with the added columns of the document titles and document links.

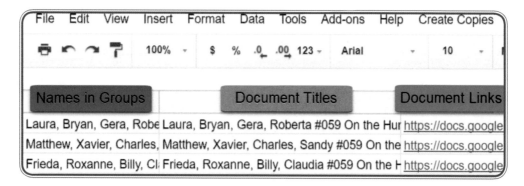

In Google Classroom, create one assignment and add all of the group Slides from Google Drive to the same assignment. Change the access from *Students can view file* to *Students can edit file*. This allows the students to edit the same document.

Learn More

Copy Docs Classes:
alicekeeler.com/copydocsclasses

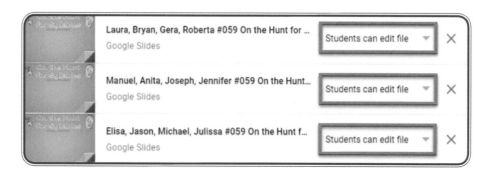

Group Docs Maker

Another approach to assigning groups of students to a group template is with an add-on located in the "Group Docs Maker" template. The add-on will randomly assign groups or allow you to determine your own groups. It creates one copy of your template per group and explicitly shares the templates with group members. This restricts other groups from accessing group documents.

In the "Group Docs Maker" template, input your students' first names, last names, and email addresses from your class roster. Use the add-on menu to choose "Group Docs Maker," and choose *Start*. After authorizing the Group Docs Maker add-on, choose from the side panel to "Make random groups" or "Make non random groups."

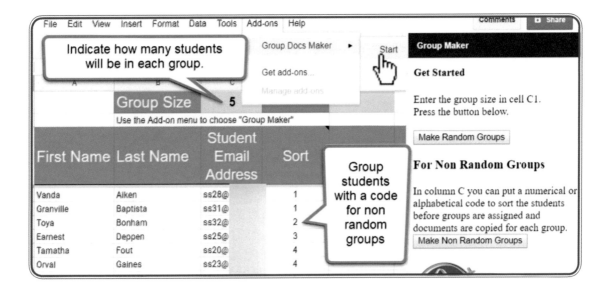

After the script is finished running, the spreadsheet will sort the students by their group code and reveal the link to the document that each group will be working in. Each group will have their own document, and only the students within those groups will be able to edit and access the document (in addition to the teacher). If a student in group 1 tries to access the document from group 3, that student will be denied access.

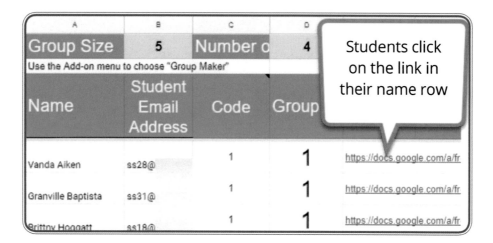

In Google Classroom, create an assignment and, from Google Drive, add the spreadsheet that has the group assignments with view-only access. Students will access their group document by opening the spreadsheet and clicking on the blue link to the document. When they are finished, they can select the blue *Mark as done* button in the Classroom assignment.

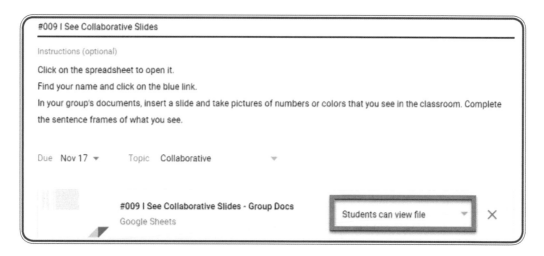

Learn More

Group Doc Maker Tutorial:
christinepinto.com/groupdocmakertutorial

Authorizing Add-ons:
alicekeeler.com/authorize

Template

Group Docs Maker:
alicekeeler.com/groupdocs

Collaborate with Upper-Grade Students

It is common for teachers to buddy up their primary students with upper elementary students and do a variety of activities together. Older students can be great coaches to Littles by modeling basic technology tasks, appropriate behavior, and more. When collaborating with technology, students do not have to be on separate devices. They can share a single device and create together.

Littles can get practice working collaboratively with their older buddies while the older students build their confidence in teaching others. This creates a win–win for both age groups. Upper-grade buddies and Littles can participate in "Getting to Know Our Buddies" slides, where they share some facts about themselves and what their favorites are. Students can organize themselves based on the colored text placeholders for them to type their responses.

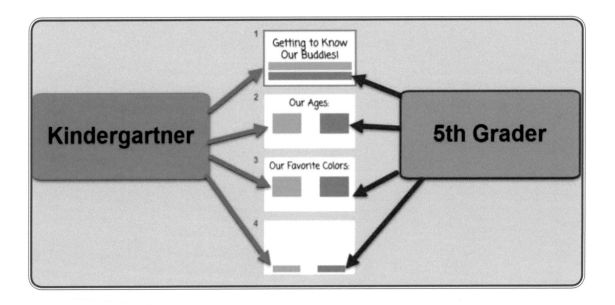

In these collaborative slides, students have designated colored areas to work in, so both the Little and the older student are contributing. Littles can type their names, numbers, and sight words. The Littles work in the green spaces and the older students work in the purple spaces. Students search for images that go along with their responses and include them in the slides. A few slide layouts were provided for student to share their names, ages, and favorite colors. Another layout with no text was included for the kids to share anything they wanted about themselves—favorite movie, sport, hobby, or place to eat. A blank Slide layout gave them the freedom to choose what they wanted to discuss. The students can choose to add slides if they want.

> **Template**
>
> **Getting to Know Our Buddies Slides**:
> christinepinto.com/buddies

Collaborate in Google Sheets

Introducing Littles to spreadsheets exposes them to a tool they can benefit from for many years to come. Using Google Sheets for group activities allows students to practice essential, real-world skills, in terms of both learning to use spreadsheets and learning to collaborate. Google Sheets is great for collaboration because multiple students can enter information into their own cell or their own sheet within the spreadsheet.

All students in the class can work on one spreadsheet. Create a blank spreadsheet and share in Google Classroom as *Students can edit file*. Spreadsheets are giant tables; each student can select a cell and share an idea and everyone can see the response. Ask students to select a cell and type their favorite color, their relation to their heroes (grandma, dad, coach, etc.), or other responses to a prompt. As the teacher, you can cut and paste student responses into organized lists to look for patterns in student responses. Add another sheet by clicking the + icon in the bottom left. Ask students to go to the next tab to share what they know about a different prompt.

Some essential spreadsheet skills are knowing how to

- Increase the width of a column
- Increase the height of a row
- Set word wrapping
- Add additional sheets

DiscussionTab

Use the "DiscussionTab" template to facilitate a discussion with the class. Although the students will discuss verbally, providing initial responses into the spreadsheet allows students time to think about their answer, learn from everyone in the class, and show patterns of responses. These data can be used to facilitate the discussion. In column A of the first sheet, type your list of discussion questions. In column B, optionally, type the name of the tab.

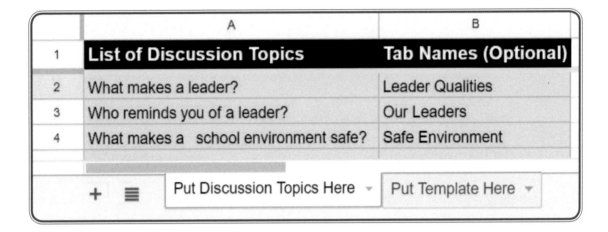

	A	B
1	**List of Discussion Topics**	**Tab Names (Optional)**
2	What makes a leader?	Leader Qualities
3	Who reminds you of a leader?	Our Leaders
4	What makes a school environment safe?	Safe Environment

Put Discussion Topics Here ▾   Put Template Here ▾

Using the DiscussionTab menu, run DiscussionTab and authorize the script. A new sheet will be created for each question, the question clearly displayed on the sheet, and the cells resized to allow for room to input longer answers. Share in Google Classroom as *Students can edit file.*

Template

Discussion spreadsheet:
alicekeeler.com/discussiontab

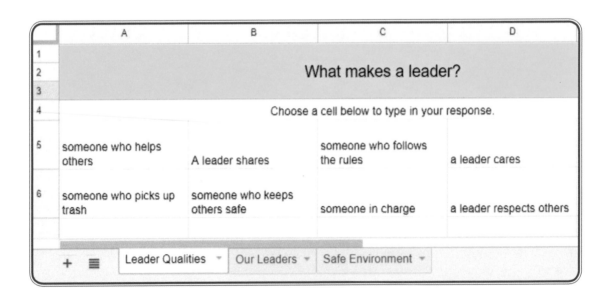

	A	B	C	D
1				
2		What makes a leader?		
3				
4		Choose a cell below to type in your response.		
5	someone who helps others	A leader shares	someone who follows the rules	a leader cares
6	someone who picks up trash	someone who keeps others safe	someone in charge	a leader respects others

Leader Qualities ▾   Our Leaders ▾   Safe Environment ▾

TemplateTab

Design your own graphic organizer with the "TemplateTab" template. On the first sheet, enter your roster of student names and, optionally, their email addresses. On the second sheet, design a graphic organizer for students. Use the TemplateTab menu to *Run TemplateTab*. This will create a copy of the graphic organizer for every student within the same spreadsheet.

> ## Template
>
> **TemplateTab:**
> alicekeeler.com/templatetab

For example, in the "Can, Have, and Are" template, the class can work in one spreadsheet but have a sheet that contains their own Can, Have, and Are graphic organizer. In the sheet titled "Put Template Here," you would type the topic in the yellow cell and leave the other cells blank for the kids to add in their information.

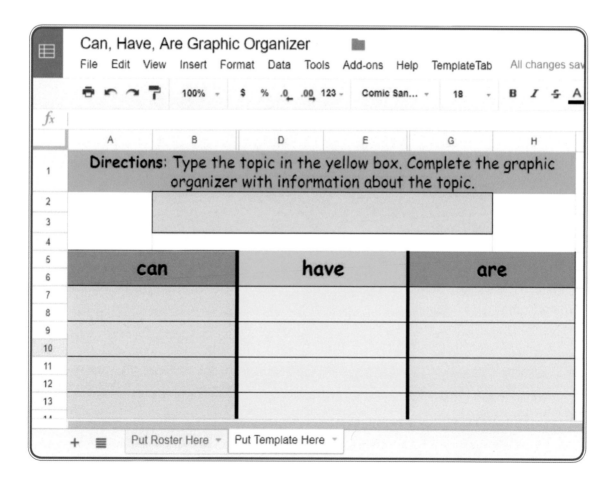

For this collaborative activity, paste your roster of student names into column A of the first sheet. From the menu: click *TemplateTab* (located next to the *Help* menu), select *Run TemplateTab* to authorize and run the add-on, and create a tab for each student.

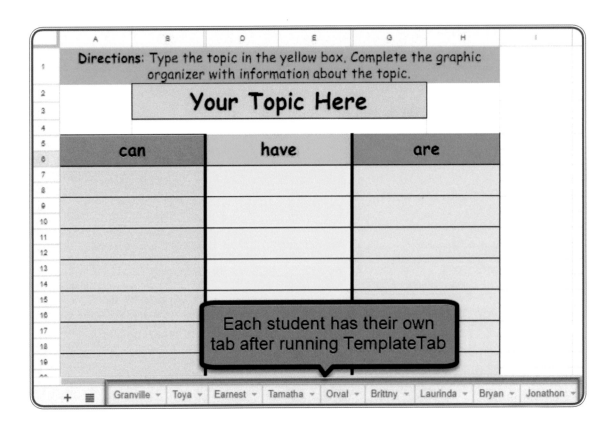

In Google Classroom, link to the collaborative spreadsheet. Change the access settings from *Students can view file* to *Students can edit file.* This gives all of the students the ability to edit the same spreadsheet. Students will open the spreadsheet and locate their name on a tab at the bottom.

Template

Can, Have, and Are Graphic Organizer: christinepinto.com/canhaveare

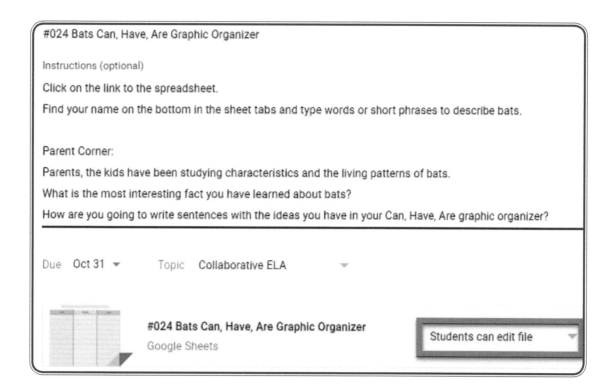

> #024 Bats Can, Have, Are Graphic Organizer
>
> Instructions (optional)
> Click on the link to the spreadsheet.
> Find your name on the bottom in the sheet tabs and type words or short phrases to describe bats.
>
> Parent Corner:
> Parents, the kids have been studying characteristics and the living patterns of bats.
> What is the most interesting fact you have learned about bats?
> How are you going to write sentences with the ideas you have in your Can, Have, Are graphic organizer?
>
> Due   Oct 31 ▼   Topic   Collaborative ELA   ▼
>
> #024 Bats Can, Have, Are Graphic Organizer
> Google Sheets   Students can edit file   ▼

Collaborate in a HyperDoc

HyperDocs are changing the way many teachers facilitate learning in their classrooms. A HyperDoc is not simply a Google Doc with hyperlinks in it. A true HyperDoc involves inquiry and collaboration. Students explore the information through the HyperDoc and interact with the information right in the document. HyperDocs contain multiple, if not all, of the super-skills essential to twenty-first-century learning—communication, collaboration, critical thinking, and creativity. Lisa Highfill, Kelly Hilton, and Sarah Landis, the creators of HyperDocs, share their knowledge in their book, *The HyperDoc Handbook*, and on Twitter using the hashtag #HyperDocs.

Learn More

Resources and information about HyperDocs and digital lesson design:
hyperdocs.co

HyperDocs will vary based on learning objectives and activities that you have in mind for students to engage in. While working with HyperDocs, Littles will typically spend their time discussing ideas with a peer, gathering information—whether from an article or gleaned from an informational video—and applying their knowledge with an activity of some sort at the end.

Many of the primary Common Core English Language Arts standards require that students identify various features of a text and specific story elements. Take your students beyond the standard. One of the first-grade Common Core ELA standards requires students to identify who is telling the story at various points in a text. Authors will sometimes put text that is being spoken by a character in a specific color, font, or size; for example, in *We Are in a Book!*, author, Mo Willems, puts Gerald the elephant's words in a gray speech bubble and Piggy's words in a pink speech bubble. Students would be thrilled to have the opportunity to be an author of a story. In the "Who Is Telling the Story" HyperDoc, kids grab a partner and click on the link to one of the stories to listen and pay attention to which characters are telling the story.

They go on to discuss how they know which character is talking when, and then have the opportunity to create a story together in Google Slides. When creating the story, the kids have complete ownership in selecting characters, developing a storyline, and determining how they are going to show readers which characters are talking at different times.

This activity takes Littles beyond identifying what they know to *applying* it to their own creation. They are creating their story from scratch, so they do not need to have a template. On the last slide, the students will share how a reader would be able to tell who is speaking in their story. They will also share their story with another pair of students, so they can get feedback about whether their story is clear.

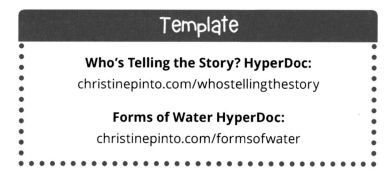

Template

Who's Telling the Story? HyperDoc:
christinepinto.com/whostellingthestory

Forms of Water HyperDoc:
christinepinto.com/formsofwater

Breakout EDU

Games are motivating for students—especially when they work in teams and tackle a challenge together. James Sanders and Adam Bellow are the founders of Breakout EDU, which is the immersive learning games platform that involves kids working collaboratively to solve critical thinking puzzles to unlock a box. The Breakout EDU website has more than 250 games with instructions on how to facilitate a Breakout. A kit that has a variety of resettable items needed to set up the games can be purchased. There are also templates and tools for educators to design their own Breakout EDU game with Google Apps or other tools.

Learn More

Breakout EDU: breakoutedu.com

Official Template to Design Your Own Game:
breakoutedu.com/create

Oompa Loompa Breakout EDU-Pinto Style

Pinto's Perspective

I read *Charlie and the Chocolate Factory* to my class and they were hooked on the plot. When they watched the original movie, it brought the story to life. The magic continued when an Oompa Loompa brought a challenge with a locked-up surprise in a treasure chest for the kids. The kids needed to work in groups to answer a question, because each group's answer revealed a digit to the code for the lock. I designed the game in Google Sheets and applied conditional formatting to the cells where students would be typing answers to indicate whether an answer was correct or incorrect. In Google Classroom, the spreadsheet with the questions was assigned as Students can edit the file. Each group only used one device, so the kids would collaborate on response options and share the device.

QUESTIONS		ANSWERS GO HERE		CODE FOR THE LOCK
#1	10 is the magic number. I'm looking for a certain number sentence to make 10.	2+8=10		**3**
#2	Words words words. A special sight word is 4 letters. Which one is it?	they		**9**
#3	In a place where you find a lot of numbers, you will find this number in the 5th column.	55		**3**
#4	Names are wonderful, every single one. How many letters are in <u>all</u> of your names put together?	45		**9**

Learn More

Oompa Loompa Breakout EDU: christinepinto.com/oompaloompa

Chapter 6
Graphing in Google Sheets

Spreadsheets. Maybe you cringe at that word. Or you might have read the word and thought, "I don't even use spreadsheets." Alternatively, you may be giggly and excited because you know the awesome things that can be done in a spreadsheet. I never thought about using spreadsheets until I met the queen of spreadsheets, Alice. Now I wonder how I went through my K–12 education without being exposed to spreadsheets and am sure to include them in my Littles' learning activities.

Early learners can classify objects, so let's display their results on a spreadsheet. One way for Littles to complete this task is physically graphing counting bears or another item and transferring the information to a Google Sheets document. There is no need to dispose of manipulatives—kids need hands-on learning experiences. So why not use manipulatives and technology together? By exposing kids to working with spreadsheets, you are giving them *another* way to organize and represent data. This physical form of graphing and transferring to the spreadsheet paves the way for more critical thinking opportunities, such as analyzing the data in a chart or table.

Combine Technology and Manipulatives

The "Graphing Bears" template is similar to the "Pixel Art" template. When students type something in the cell, the cell fills with color. The difference with this Google Sheets template is that the cell color fills according to bear color, which is based on the column; for example, when a letter or number is typed in the column for the yellow bears, the cell will turn yellow. As students fill the cells, the number of filled cells automatically generates in the row underneath the table for each column of bears.

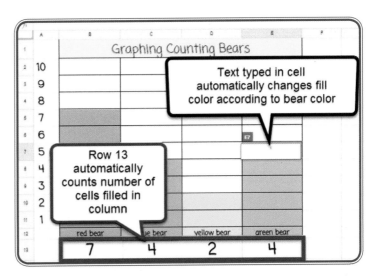

Learn More

More Details about Exploring Graphing Template:

alicekeeler.com/ksheets

Template

Exploring Graphing— 4 Different Samples:

alicekeeler.com/exploringgraphing

Graph the Weather

Students often work with numbers or problems that are given to them, but students tune in and are more engaged when they feel involved and can contribute to an activity. Empower your Littles by allowing them to collect their own data. This is a task the entire class can do together to learn as a group.

One of the Next Generation Science Standards states that students can use and share observations of local weather conditions to describe patterns that occur over time. Students can rotate the role of being the weather reporter daily or weekly. The weather reporter can poke his or her head outside to check out the weather and record the weather details in a Google Sheet because each month has a copy of the weather chart. This means every month's weather chart is in one spreadsheet, making it easy to access and compare and contrast all the data.

A Step Further

The weather can vary depending on where you are in the world. For kids who may not have traveled out of their region, they might not know how weather can vary based on location! I teach in southern California, where it we see mostly sunny skies with a few showers during winter and spring. Some of my students are "mind blown" to know that it snows in other places.

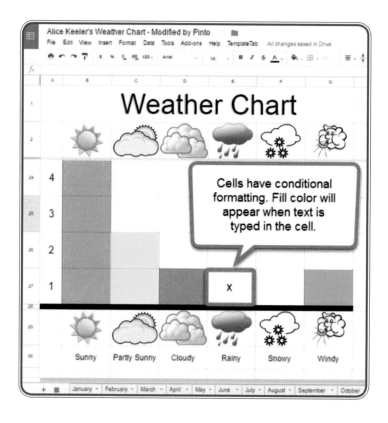

Modern technology allows us to easily have video conversations with people in various locations. Consider inviting educators whose classes are in different regions from where you teach to participate in charting the weather. Virtually "meet up" on occasion to compare and contrast weather charts and experiences that come with the different weather types. Share this interest of yours with your professional learning network and on social media (Twitter is a great place to find educators) to connect with another teacher. Alternatively, students may have family members who live outside of your region and can share what the weather is like. There are ways to make this experience happen!

Template

Weather Chart:
alicekeeler.com/weatherchart

Create Your Own Weather Chart

To create a template like the weather chart, you need to know a few simple spreadsheet functions. First, freezing the first row. Use the *View* menu to choose *Freeze*, select *1 frozen row*.

Notice the title "Weather Chart" is a merged group of cells. Highlight several cells and use the *merge* icon in the toolbar to convert to one large cell. The *merge* icon looks like a symbol for elevator doors that are closing.

Inserting images into a spreadsheet cell requires the formula =IMAGE("URL"). Locate an image on the web that you have permission to use and right click. In the Chrome browser you will have the option to *Copy image address*. Other browsers will also have an option to obtain the image URL but may use slightly different verbiage. In the cell where you would like the image to appear, start with an equals sign and type the word *IMAGE* followed by an open parenthesis. Before pasting the link to the image, type a quotation mark. The Image address (URL) will need to be in quotations. Include the closing parenthesis and press *ENTER*.

Conditional formatting is achieved by highlighting the cells that will be filled in with color in response to student input. From the *Format* menu, choose *Conditional formatting*. This will produce a sidebar for you to set the formatting options on the selected range. Change the condition from *Cell is empty* to *Cell is not empty*. Also in the sidebar is the option to set the fill color and the font color if the condition is met. For this activity, you must ensure that the fill color and font color match. This way, when students type any value into the cell, what they type will disappear and the cell will be filled with color.

Learn More

Create Your Own Weather Chart Tutorial:
christinepinto.com/createweatherchart

Manipulate a Google Drawing

On a computer platform, a Google Drawing can be inserted into a spreadsheet in Google Sheets. The drawing acts like a floating image that can be moved anywhere on the spreadsheet. Students could have a drawing that goes along with their data. In the "Leaves on My Tree" template, students double click on the tree, which is the drawing, and can move the leaves that are on the left and place them on the tree. The leaves are in stacks, meaning the leaves are on top of each other. When the student moves a leaf, there is another leaf underneath it. Students can add leaves to the tree, and click *Save & close* to save their drawings.

Afterward, students will graph the number and colors of leaves they have on their trees. When any text is typed in one of the columns, it will automatically change the fill color of the cell. When students complete the graph, they will complete sentences about how many leaves they have by typing in a number that corresponds with their graph and leaves on the tree.

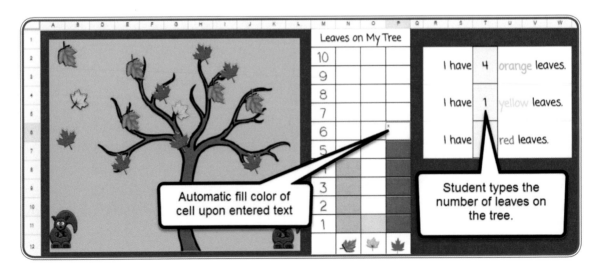

Template

Google Sheets templates where students manipulate items in a Google Drawing, graph the items they manipulated, and complete sentence frames:

christinepinto.com/leavesonmytree   christinepinto.com/leprechaunscene

christinepinto.com/halloweenscene   christinepinto.com/fishbowl

christinepinto.com/ornamentsonmytree   christinepinto.com/scatteredeggs

christinepinto.com/winterscenegraph

Create Pie Charts

Google Sheets allows Littles to create pie charts, which allows them to analyze information. In the "Pie Charts Activity" template, they start out by typing their names in a cell, which then reveals a pie chart with a table of numbers to manipulate. The kids will change a number and see that the pie pieces will either get larger or smaller, depending on the other numbers of the other pieces. A space is provided for students to share their observations before being prompted to go to the next sheet.

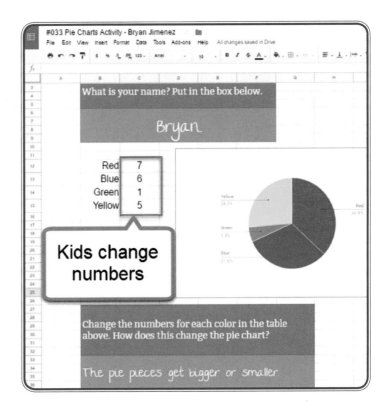

In the second sheet titled "Compare," students are presented with two graphs in which they can change the numbers in the tables. They can then share the differences they notice between the two pie charts.

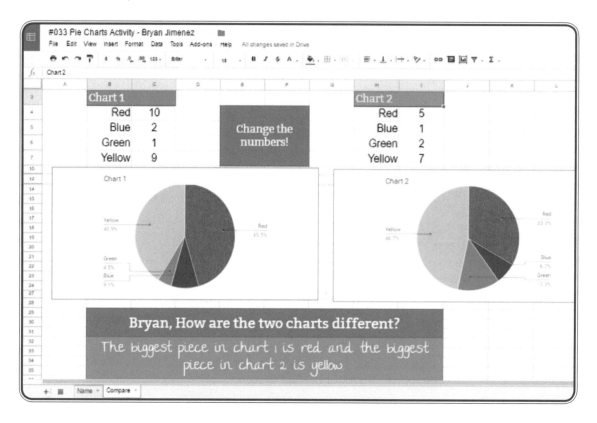

Template

Pie Charts Activity:
alicekeeler.com/piechartsactivity

Chapter 7
Tech Tools to Support ELA

Littles can use technology even as they are building their foundational reading skills. A good digital lesson plan involves working toward a learning goal while using technology. One of the benefits of integrating technology is that students can explore and express themselves and their knowledge with creativity. As a result, technology tools allow each of your students' projects to be unique and original. In addition to G Suite, many other tools out there can support Littles in the creation and learning process. Here are a few tools and methods we recommend for building English and Language Arts skills:

Google Classroom Private Comments

One place to start with using technology to support students' writing skills is with *Private comments* in Google Classroom. Every assignment automatically creates a spot for students to respond in with *Private comments*. Having no documents to manage makes this a quick way to interact with students and improve their learning. Ask students to write something in the *Private comments* that addresses a specific learning objective. When clicking on the assignment title in Google Classroom, you are able to find a roster of student names and their responses. Click on each name to view the student response. In the *Private comments*, provide a response to each student that is specific and actionable. How can they improve on their writing? Ask students to rewrite their sentence(s) in response to the feedback.

Learn More

Video Feedback Sample:
goo.gl/d826dX

Alice Keeler Webcam Record Chrome extension:
alicekeeler.com/webcam

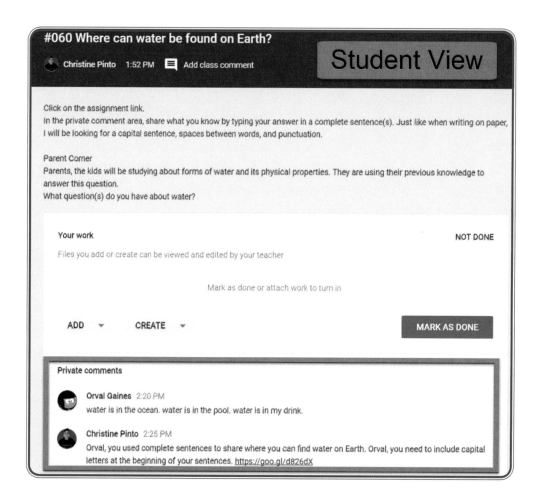

Student View

#060 Where can water be found on Earth?

Christine Pinto   1:52 PM   Add class comment

Click on the assignment link.
In the private comment area, share what you know by typing your answer in a complete sentence(s). Just like when writing on paper, I will be looking for a capital sentence, spaces between words, and punctuation.

Parent Corner
Parents, the kids will be studying about forms of water and its physical properties. They are using their previous knowledge to answer this question.
What question(s) do you have about water?

Your work   NOT DONE
Files you add or create can be viewed and edited by your teacher

Mark as done or attach work to turn in

ADD ▾   CREATE ▾   MARK AS DONE

Private comments

Orval Gaines 2:20 PM
water is in the ocean. water is in the pool. water is in my drink.

Christine Pinto 2:25 PM
Orval, you used complete sentences to share where you can find water on Earth. Orval, you need to include capital letters at the beginning of your sentences. https://goo.gl/d826dX

Keeler's Tips

Littles may be challenged to read detailed feedback about their writing. Instead of text feedback, provide video feedback using your webcam. My Webcam Record Chrome extension allows you to record thirty seconds of video. The webcam recording is saved automatically into a folder in Google Drive. One time only, go to Google Drive and change the sharing permissions of the folder to be *Anyone with the link can view*. This will allow the students to view the recording. The link to the video is automatically copied to the clipboard. Simply paste (*Control-V*) the link into the *Private comments* in Google Classroom.

Google Keep

Google Keep is a mobile app available on tablets and also can be accessed on the web. Keep is a small note-taking tool with some amazing capabilities. It allows students to brainstorm ideas and jot down quick thoughts or to-do's. Regularly ask students to use Google Keep to keep a list of what they are going to work on for the day. Students can check off items they have completed. Notes in Google Keep can also be shared with peers or the teacher.

Draw Your Vocab

Have students sketch a drawing in Google Keep to represent their understanding of vocabulary. In a Google Doc on a Chromebook or PC, students use the *Tools* menu to choose *Keep notepad*. This brings up a side panel to allow students to drag their drawing into the Google Doc.

Learn More

Google Keep: keep.google.com

Google Docs

Google Docs is probably the most obvious technology tool for use with student writing. Have students collaborate on writing together by one student sharing the document with another student. They can use different-colored fonts to distinguish who contributed what to the document.

In Docs, and many of the other Google Apps, users can leave comments for collaborators to view and respond to. This feature allows your students to add feedback on one another's work without editing the original document. To insert a comment, click, select text or an image, and click on the icon that looks like a quote bubble. Alternatively, you can use the keyboard shortcut: *Control* (*Command* on a Mac), *Alt* (*Option* on a Mac), and *M* to insert a comment. Use the *Control* and *Enter* keys to save the comment.

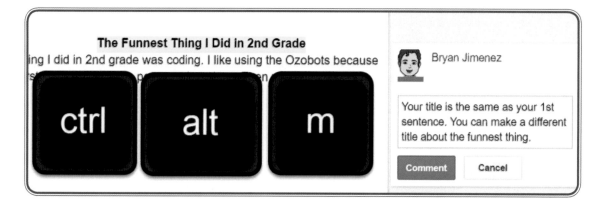

Keeler's Tips

The most powerful feedback is when students receive the feedback while they are still working on the activity rather than after they believe they are done. G Suite allows you to have access to student work from start to finish, allowing the feedback to come during the process rather than after. Expect students to respond to feedback and improve their work before submitting.

Draftback

It can be beneficial for students or teachers to go through the version history of a Google Doc. For students, it can be an activity that helps in the reflection of writing. They can see how far along they came in a writing piece, and they may want to bring back some ideas that they removed from an earlier draft. Draftback is a Chrome extension that will allow you to play back the version history of a Google Doc that you have editing access to. Draftback also can be handy for teachers, because statistics graphs are provided to show a student's activity in the Doc, such as how many revisions were made and the time spans during which students were working.

Learn More

Draftback:
christinepinto.com/draftback

Brainstorming Race

Brainstorming Race is an add-on for Google Docs that allows students to brainstorm ideas and then convert the ideas to a Google Form for voting. This tool can come in handy when students are working in groups and need to select a topic to focus on. For example, second graders learn about various animals that live in a certain habitat (NGSS 2-LS4-1). Instead of giving the kids a certain habitat to study, let the kids list habitats they would want to study, and they can vote to narrow down their choices.

Another way students can use Brainstorming Race is to collect responses from their peers and interpret data. A student can come up with a "Question of the Day" in which a student can think of a question they would like to ask the class and list possible responses that his or her peers may have. After running the Brainstorm Race add-on, the class can answer the question via the automatically generated Google Form. In the Responses tab of the Google Form, students can look back on the pie chart and discuss any patterns they see with the data of their responses.

Learn More

Brainstorming Race Add-on:
christinepinto.com/brainstormingrace

Read&Write

Texthelp is a company that leads in assistive learning software and is a partner with G Suite for Education. Read&Write for Google Chrome is a tool that provides numerous ways to support students with reading content in Google Apps, web pages, and more.

Once you've installed the Read&Write for Google Chrome extension, a tool bar of features for reading will appear above the menu items in a Google App or on top of a web page.

With the premium features, students can highlight text on web pages and collect highlights, use a picture dictionary, add a voice note, or add a screen mask, which shades out the part students are not reading.

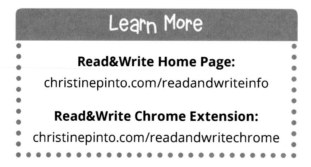

Learn More

Read&Write Home Page:
christinepinto.com/readandwriteinfo

Read&Write Chrome Extension:
christinepinto.com/readandwritechrome

Fluency Tutor

Fluency Tutor for Google is another resource that Texthelp offers to support student reading skills, and it works seamlessly with G Suite for Education and has Google Classroom integration. The tool focuses on improving students' reading aloud skills and is friendly to new readers, English-language learners, and struggling readers. The product (which offers a thirty-day free trial) allows teachers to choose content, whether a web page, created content, or preselected reading passages. It also provides the Lexile, age, and word count information for the selected material. Teachers and students can share content via Google Classroom or Google Drive. Students can read and record their passages aloud, play back their recordings, re-record if they wish, and submit their recordings to their teachers.

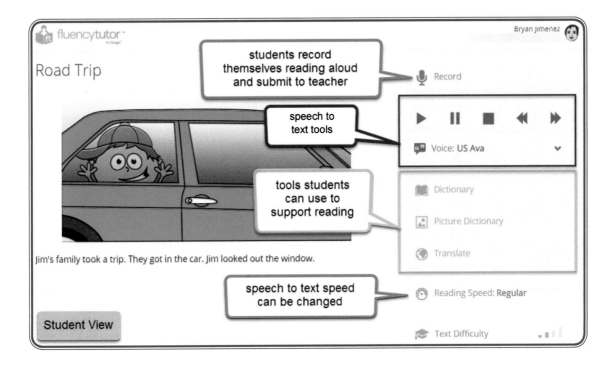

Fluency Tutor:

christinepinto.com/fluencytutor

Fluency Tutor has a teacher dashboard where you can review student submissions and keep track of which entries need to be scored. It also allows you to see which of Fluency Tutor's built-in tools students use, such as the picture dictionary and translate features. You can play back recordings with the text in front of you and score the results like a running record, listening for mispronunciations, omissions, and substitutions of words. Before submitting the reading record score, you can indicate on a one-to-four scale the student's expression, phrasing, smoothness, and pace, which are factored in with the score. Scores are automatically charted by student to monitor progress throughout the year.

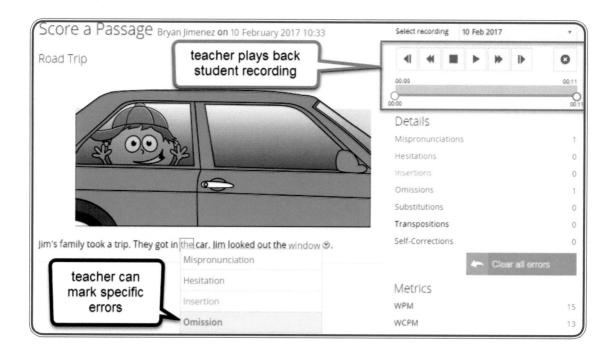

Fluency Tutor works in the Chrome browser app for PCs, Macs, and Chromebooks, in addition to the student app for Android tablets.

Sequence Writing and Sundae Building

Students as young as kindergarten are expected to compose various types of writing, such as narrative, opinion, and explanatory pieces. The writing process may start with a class discussion on a specific topic. The teacher then creates a thinking map to provide a visual and organize the students' thoughts and ideas. The goal is to help students develop an understanding of how to use thinking maps to help them with their writing.

In the "Build a Sundae" template, students first manipulate a Google Drawing in Google Docs to create an ice cream sundae. They manipulate another Google drawing to create a flow map by sequencing which items they used to create the sundae. The transition words and labels for the sundae items are part of the template and included in the Google Drawing. Finally, students use their completed flow map to type out their sentences. This activity can be varied in multiple ways; for example, when the kids are more fluent with sequence writing, they can drag their images into the flow map and develop their own sentences.

Template

Build a Sundae:
christinepinto.com/buildasundae

Build Your Own Activity
(blank version for you to add content):
christinepinto.com/buildyourown

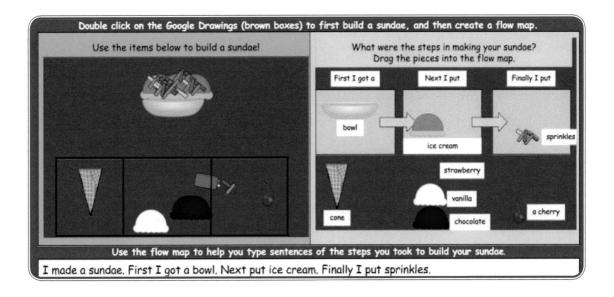

Magnetic Poetry

Creating poetry is another way students can be expressive and communicate their thoughts. Poetry gives young writers the opportunity to be creative with word selection and work outside the structure of a sentence. Kasey Bell from shakeuplearning.com created digital magnetic poetry templates with Google Drawing and Slides. Students can drag words from a word bank to the middle of the template, and they can insert text boxes to add more magnetic words to their poems. The magnetic poetry activity can be taken in a different direction by allowing students to work collaboratively within the same document, so they can build on one another's ideas.

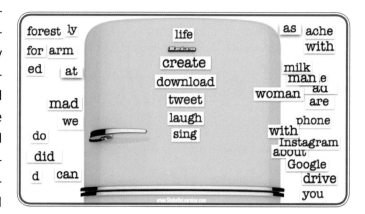

Template

Magnetic Poetry Template:
shakeuplearning.com/magnetic

Learn More

Kasey Bell's Blog Post about Magnetic Poetry:
shakeuplearning.com/magneticpoetry

Storyboarding

StoryboardThat is a digital storytelling tool that allows students to create a comic strip, infographic, or graphic organizer. The tool allows students to visually communicate or represent a skill or idea. Students can drag settings, characters, text, and other elements into their storyboards to demonstrate their understanding of a science experiment, recreate a historical scene, represent vocabulary words with graphics, create stories to practice writing, and more.

First I wake up in my room. | Next I get redy in the bathroom. | Last I et brekfast in the kitchin.

Students can create a StoryboardThat account using their Google login information. In Google Classroom, assign the link to StoryboardThat. Students will click on the link to take them to the application. After logging in and completing the storyboard, they can save their work and then link to the Google Classroom assignment.

When you introduce StoryboardThat to students, give them the freedom to explore on their own. You might have a specific idea in mind as to what you would like students to visually represent; however, the kids will be excited by the personalization features and will likely want to create their own storyboards. Giving students an opportunity to explore a new tool without directions allows them to enjoy their creations, so they can focus on more specific assignments the next time the tool is used.

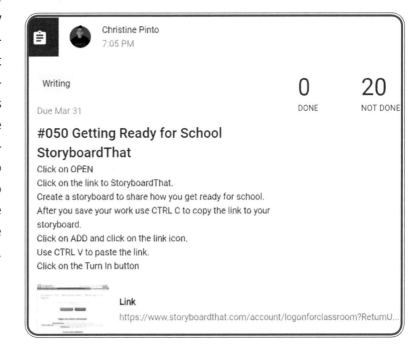

Go Beyond the Basics

Being able to identify story elements (settings, characters, events, etc.) is essential for kids' reading comprehension. To avoid redundancy in the way they identify and describe story elements, allow students to create; give them choices and be open to the different ways they choose to show you what they know about the story. Let them determine how they will address the learning objective. Your students will become fluent in using Google Apps, among other applications, and will have enough of a foundation to create with technology.

Template

Visuals in Drawing Sample Directions:
christinepinto.com/elementsindrawing

StoryboardThat Sample Directions:
christinepinto.com/elementsinstoryboard

Illustration or Model Sample Directions:
christinepinto.com/elementsinillustration

Map It Out

Technology tools such as Google Maps can allow your students to explore the world beyond the maps in an atlas or in the back of their social studies book—without ever leaving the classroom. To access Google Maps, go to maps.google.com. In Google Classroom, use the link icon to link to Google Maps and just let the kids explore. Allow them to click around, zoom in, and be free to discover. After a time, discuss with the kids what they saw in the Google Map, what they discovered, and what they figured out how to do.

Due Jan 25

#030 Exploring Google Maps
Click on the link and click on the CREATE button.
Title your map and EXPLORE in the map! Click on the different icons to see what they do.
Choose a way to share what you discovered:
- Type in the private comment area. Then click MARK AS DONE.
- Click on CREATE and select Docs to voice type.
- Use a screencast tool to capture your response while talking.
- Use the SlideShot extension to take pictures AS you're exploring.

Sign in - Google Accounts
http://mymaps.google.com

During the exploration phase, students will likely try to find places with which they can relate or are familiar. A good way to spark their curiosity is to use the "Special Place on the Map" activity. The kids can listen to the reading of *Me on the Map* by Joan Sweeney, where the main character accesses multiple resources to locate her special place on the map. Students can choose a special place and see what it looks like from multiple views or perspectives in Google Maps.

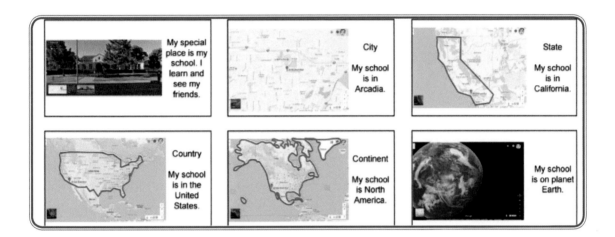

Have students use the zooming features in Google Maps to view locations from space all the way down to the street level. Students can take screenshots as they are zooming in or out to view their special place up close or from a distance. iPad users take a screenshot by holding down the Home button and the power button at the same time. This adds the screenshot to the camera roll, which can easily be inserted into a Google Slides presentation.

The Alice Keeler SlideShot Chrome extension comes in handy with this activity. Chrome extensions can only be used with a Chromebook or a PC with the Chrome browser. After installing SlideShot, its icon will appear in the Chrome extension shelf. Students click on the icon and choose *Start*. This automatically creates and saves a screenshot every minute. Students can also take screenshots manually with the extension by clicking on the icon and choosing *Manual capture*. Clicking *Finish* in the SlideShot extension will automatically create a Google Slides presentation of the screenshots, which is saved in Google Drive. All screenshots that were taken in the duration that the extension was being used are also available in Google Drive on finishing. Each slide contains the screenshot as well as a text box to allow the students to describe the image. Students can choose which screenshots they want to keep or delete. At the end of the slides, the kids can share why they chose that particular place and why it is special to them. In Google Classroom, students can use the *Add* button in an assignment to select their Google Slides activity from Google Drive to turn in.

Learn More

Special Place on Earth Directions:
christinepinto.com/specialplace

SlideShot Chrome Extension:
alicekeeler.com/slideshot

Collaborative Maps

Mymaps.google.com can also be used to create custom maps for students, where they can work collaboratively within the same map. The maps are saved to Google Drive and allow students to insert pins or draw lines to describe different places on the map. This tool can spark opportunities for students to work across content areas. For example, if second-grade students are studying living things, they can map out the different places those living things exist and make observations based on the locations of the living things (2-LS4-1). Students can document the locations on the collaborative Google My Maps and record information they discovered right in the map, Google Docs, or another platform familiar to them.

Sharing a My Maps

Create a new map at mymaps.google.com and title it. In My Maps, layers can be used as a way to organize information students input on the map. Add a layer for however students are going to be grouped, whether it is a whole class collaboration (each group gets a layer) or a small group collaboration (each individual person gets a layer). When you create the assignment, add the Google My Maps by clicking on the *Drive* icon and selecting the map. Be sure to give students editing access to the map, so they can make additions to it.

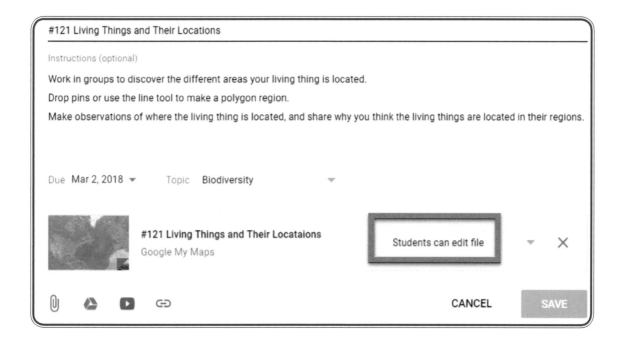

Chapter 8
Tech Resources to Support Mathematics

It is not uncommon for students to struggle with math; rote worksheets can give the impression that math is dry, and students can struggle to make real-life connections. Jo Boaler, Stanford professor of mathematics, states in her book *Mathematical Mindsets* that math is creative and visual. She also points out that making mistakes is a valuable part of the learning process, and valuing different approaches helps students to appreciate mathematics beyond procedural steps. Google Apps can help students to take a creative and visual approach to math.

Learn More

Mathematical Mindsets by Jo Boaler:
alicekeeler.com/mathmindsets

Clearly Communicate Ideas

Google Slides is an excellent tool for students modeling their math. Students can use physical manipulatives and use the webcam or tablet to insert a picture of their manipulative onto a slide. Students can also use the drawing tools right in Google Slides to represent their ideas for mathematics. Go beyond finding the answer and include clearly communicating ideas and strategies. Have students add a text box to communicate their strategy. Although no template is needed, students can independently add a text box; however, when templates are provided, consider using a text placeholder to add a strategy box for the students.

Share Your Strategy Template

In the "Share Your Strategy" template, the students add a slide to show their math. Notice the text box provided to allow the students to communicate their thinking. Students should be discouraged from editing or deleting their "mistakes." With Google Slides, students can easily add another slide and try another strategy or approach. The text box allows the student to explain how they developed their thinking.

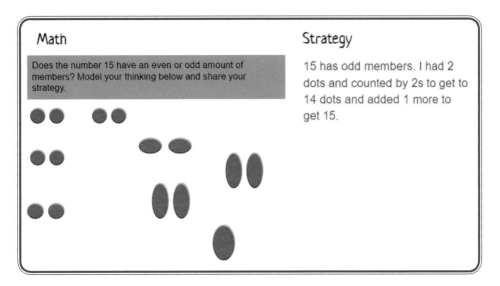

Instead of a text box, students can insert a video explaining their thinking into the Google Slide. Students can record a video and save it to Google Drive. From a PC or Chromebook, the students can insert a video from Google Drive.

Template

Share Your Strategy:
alicekeeler.com/shareyourstrategy

Share one Google Slides with edit access with all of the students and have them each add a slide with their visualization of a math problem. This allows students to value the approaches of others and to see that there is not just one way to visualize or complete a math problem. One of the eight mathematical principles is to "critique the reasoning of others." When students work together on the same Slides presentation, they are able to insert comments to ask questions about the different approaches their classmates used. Clicking the *Present* button allows for all student ideas to be easily shared and discussed with the class.

In addition to students using the same Google Slides, students can each work on their own copy. Rather than focusing on the procedural steps to come up with an answer, ask students to try to solve a problem multiple ways. A student would add multiple slides to the presentation to work on the same problem. For each slide the student would include a description of each of their varied strategies.

> ## Template
>
> **Collaborative Strategies:**
> christinepinto.com/collaborativestrategies

> ## Keeler's Tips
>
>
>
> Use the Chrome extension EquatIO to have students insert math symbols and expressions into Google Docs, Slides, and Forms. The premium version supports voice typing of math, handwriting conversion, and inclusion in Google Slides and Forms.
>
> **EquatIO Chrome Extension:** alicekeeler.com/equatio

Faster Feedback

We've said it before: technology for technology's sake isn't the goal. Simply substituting a digital format for a paper format in any subject does not improve learning. But you *can* use technology to greatly improve on the traditional mathematics worksheet. Rather than simply posting digital worksheets online for students to fill out, consider ways to increase student–teacher interaction; for example, one way technology can make learning better is by providing students with immediate feedback. Timely feedback increases motivation and prevents students from practicing a method incorrectly.

Using a Spreadsheet for Immediate Feedback

Spreadsheets can also offer the opportunity for students to get immediate feedback on their work. If the question has a specific answer, let the computer grade it! Use conditional formatting in a spreadsheet to check answers. Create an answer box in the spreadsheet. Right click on the cell, or use the Format menu, and choose *Conditional formatting*. In the sidebar, select *Answer is exactly* or *Is equal to* from the drop-down menu. Below the menu, enter the solution to the math problem. Choose the fill color the student will see if they answer correctly. If the student answers incorrectly, the cell will not change color.

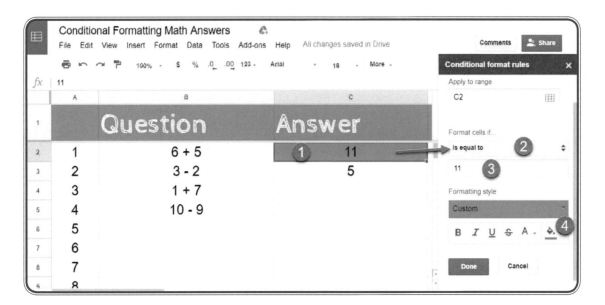

Understanding how tabs work in a spreadsheet is a valuable skill. Create each question on its own sheet. This allows you to insert drawings of visuals along with an answer box. Students would move to the next tab to answer the next question.

Learn More

Conditional Formatting Sample Sheet:
alicekeeler.com/cfsample

Keeler's Tips

Math symbols for Littles can sometimes be tricky to add. The division symbol, for example, is difficult to insert. Here are some suggestions for adding math symbols to Sheets:

- Copy and paste symbols from the web.
- Use the Chrome extension EquatIO to insert math symbols.
- Take screenshots of math problems and insert drawings onto the sheet.

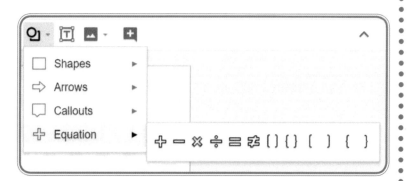

Check My Answer Template

With the "Check My Answer Spreadsheet Worksheet" template, you can enter questions and create an answer key. Click on the tiny triangle on the Answer Key sheet and select *Hide sheet* so students do not see the answers.

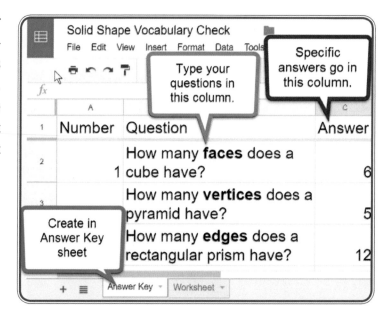

When students type their answers into the "Worksheet" sheet, conditional formatting in the spreadsheet provides students with immediate feedback by turning the cell green if their answer is correct.

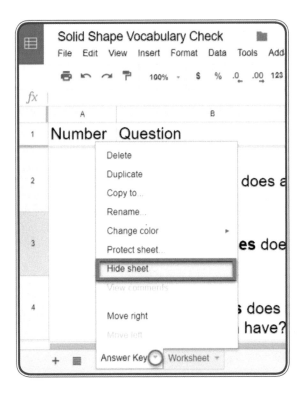

Template

Spreadsheet Worksheet:
alicekeeler.com/worksheet

Spreadsheet Worksheet Game:
alicekeeler.com/worksheetgame

Learn More

Formative: goformative.com

Desmos: Desmos.com

Quizziz: quizizz.com

That Quiz: thatquiz.org

Quia: quia.com/web

Socrative: socrative.com

Kahoot: getkahoot.com

Sugarcane:
sugarcane.com/topic/math

IXL Math: ixl.com

Digital Feedback

A number of websites allow you to ask students questions digitally so they get immediate feedback. Choose a digital tool that does the grading for you. After entering the answer to the question, the computer immediately tells the student if the answer is correct or not. This allows you, the teacher, to spend more time meaningfully working with students rather than grading. When a student is not being successful, they know it before completing an entire set of problems. Unlike paper worksheets, students can practice until they are successful rather than having to complete a certain number of problems regardless of whether they need to.

Models and Equations Activities

At the primary level, students are expected to comprehend the meaning of the equals sign. In a Google Sheet, starting with an equals sign allows students to calculate math expressions and check their work.

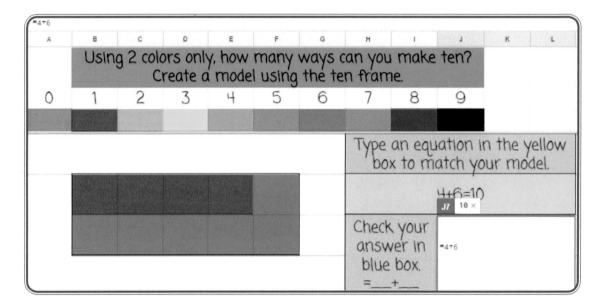

In the "Models and Equation" template, students use paint-by-number pixel art to model that two groups combine to make five in a five-frame and ten in a ten-frame. Students type single-digit numbers into the five- or ten-frames to color the cells. The numbers correlate to a color. After modeling the math, the students write an equation such as 3 + 7 = 10 in the yellow cell. To check their answers, the students type = 3 + 7 into the blue spreadsheet cell to verify that it indeed adds up to 10.

Older primary students can make arrays (an arrangement of items) of twenty to demonstrate an understanding of creating equations to show the total as a sum of equal addends (numbers that are added together). Some arrays can potentially have two equations; the template allows students to ponder whether their array can have another equation and type it out. A space is provided in the template for students to share their thinking.

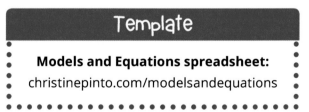

Template

Models and Equations spreadsheet:
christinepinto.com/modelsandequations

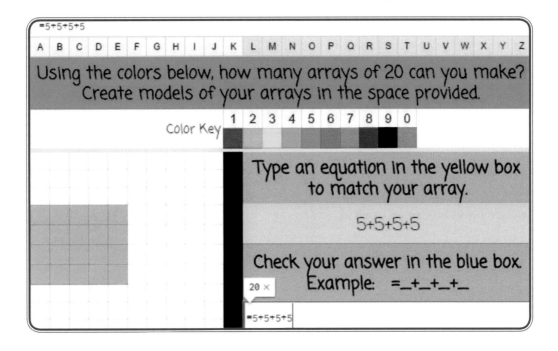

Sorting Shapes

Classifying objects is a skill that little kids acquire early on. In this activity, students examine a group of objects that have various attributes and determine how to sort them. In the "Shape Sorting Google Slides" templates, students are presented images to sort. The "Level 1 Shape Sort" template has circles and triangles of different sizes around the perimeter of the slide. The students determine how they would like to sort the shapes by clicking and dragging them to either side of the center line.

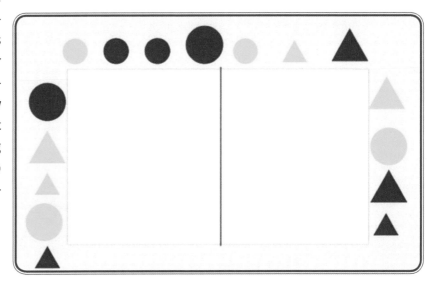

Before they get started, have students click on the View menu and select the *50%* view so they can see all of the objects around the Slide. (The trick to designing a template like this is to put the objects in the Off Canvas space, which is the light gray area next to the Slide, but you will need to change the view to see the Off Canvas space.)

When students are finished sorting, they can move on to the next Slide and sort the objects again in a different way.

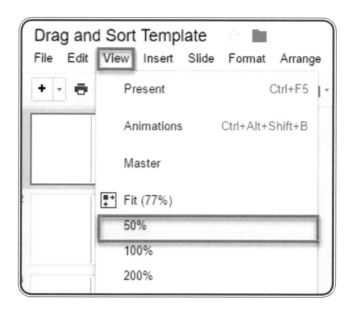

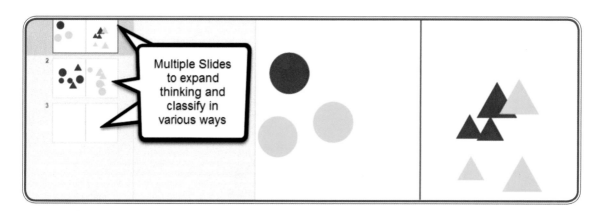

Multiple Slides to expand thinking and classify in various ways

Templates

Level 1 Shape Sort—
Circles and Triangles:
alicekeeler.com/slidesdragandsort

Level 2 Shape Sort—
Triangles and Quadrilaterals:
christinepinto.com/level2shapesort

Level 3 Shape Sort—3D Shapes:
christinepinto.com/3dsort

Composite 2D Shapes

It is okay for students to be working on a meaningful assignment for a substantial amount of time, if the time spent increases their understanding and digital literacy skills. Sometimes you might come up with an activity, or be inspired by someone else's idea, and realize that it needs to be broken down into a few sub-lessons for your students. Do not hold back on an activity because of time! It is more beneficial for students to spend their time on a task, problem solving and thinking critically, than working on an assignment that can be completed within minutes and involves low levels of thinking. It often helps to plan with an end product in mind. Think of it as if your lessons are *building* on each other.

Open Middle is a website that provides higher critical thinking sample math problems. In an Open Middle activity by Bryan Anderson, students are asked to identify as many shapes as possible in a composite shape of a house. The possible answers should exceed the actual shapes used to create the picture initially. This depth of knowledge level 2 (DOK 2) activity can be enhanced by Google Apps by having students create the shapes. The next three activities can be completed in isolation; however, we think the lessons complement each other.

Class Chat on Composite Shapes

Technology gives teachers the ability to facilitate a whole-class discussion *and* have each student participate. Instead of talking to the class and getting five kids to raise their hands and share their knowledge, each student can have the opportunity to contribute with a collaborative learning tool.

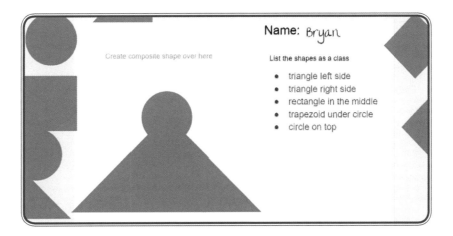

In the "Class Chat on Composite Shapes" template, students have an opportunity to work in the collaborative slides template and practice creating their own composite shape. During this activity, the students slide and drag the shapes that are in the gray canvas space onto the slide to have them overlap and become a composite shape. Afterward, hold a whole-class discussion about the shapes they can spot in their classmates' composite shapes. With an all-class collaboration, students are able to hear from their peers about hidden shapes that they might not have thought of, especially the less obvious shapes.

Template

Class Chat on Composite Shapes:
alicekeeler.com/compositecollaborate

Polyline Tool Activity

After the kids have explored the construction of a composite shape, an ideal activity involves having the kids draw shapes on a composite shape. Trying to insert shapes on top of a composite shape and making it exactly the way they want can be challenging for students; however, drawing their own shape on the composite shape would result in an easier time. The polyline tool is what your students will need to use for this activity. If your students have not worked with the polyline tool before, have them take some time to explore it before trying to draw their own shape inside a composite shape.

In the "Polyline Tool Activity" template, the first slides serve as blank canvas to draw a shape, change the fill color, and make the outline of the shape transparent. These are skills that students need to know how to apply for other digital features, such as images and text boxes,

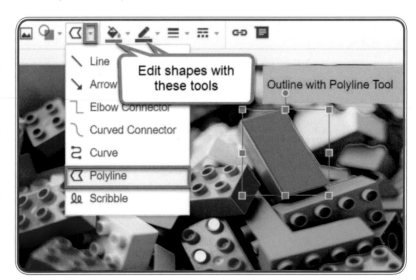

when designing. After the kids draw some shapes with the polyline, they can move on to the slides with images and practice outlining using the polyline tool. Likely the kids will try to find shapes within the images and outline shapes without you having to tell them.

This activity becomes more engaging for the kids when their interests are set as the backgrounds on the slides. Survey your students' opinions for which images they would like to have included in the activity. After you have made a copy of the template, click on the *View* menu and select *Master*. You will see a number of premade master slide layouts that you can edit. To insert a new master slide layout with your students' interest, click in between two slides and hit the *Enter* key. When the slide appears, click on the *Background* button, select *Image*, and search for an image from your students' suggestions.

Template

Polyline Tool Activity:
alicekeeler.com/polyline

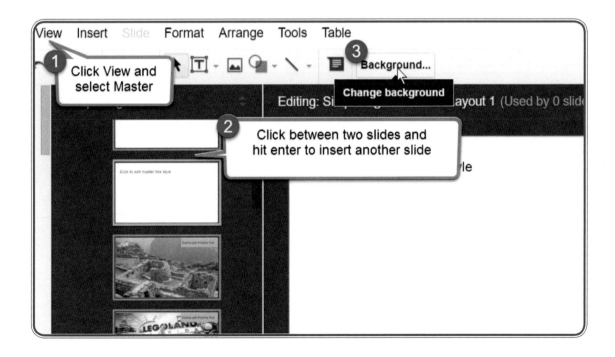

Partner Activity on Composite Shapes

When your students are familiar with creating shapes with the polyline tool, they can apply this skill to the Partner Activity on Composite Shapes. In this activity, each kid in a pair begins by working in the "Blank Google Slides" template (assigned in Google Classroom) and accessing the Slide Master, which is located under the *View* menu. When students create in the Slide Master, the design or content on the Slide Master is locked down and will not move in the filmstrip of the slides where students will be working. The tricks to creating a composite shape are overlapping the shapes and making the borderline transparent.

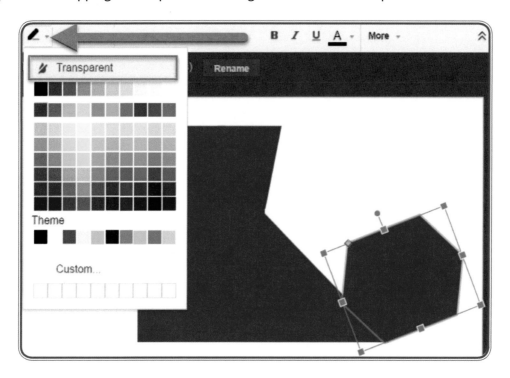

After the students create their composite shapes, they will click on the blue Share button and type in their partner's email address.

Alternatively, you can create a new Google Classroom assignment and link all of the students' Google Slides presentations and assign them as *Students can edit* files. Create a new assignment and link to student files by clicking on the *Drive* icon and search the title assignment. This is where the hashtag system definitely comes in handy, because you would only have to search the hashtag with the assignment number and all of the files with that hashtag would appear.

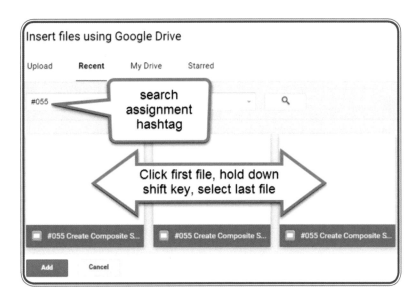

By including all of the student files in the Google Classroom assignment, students have access to one another's Google Slides presentations. This allows them to have automatic sharing permissions to their partner's Google Slides, because the files are assigned as *Students can edit* files.

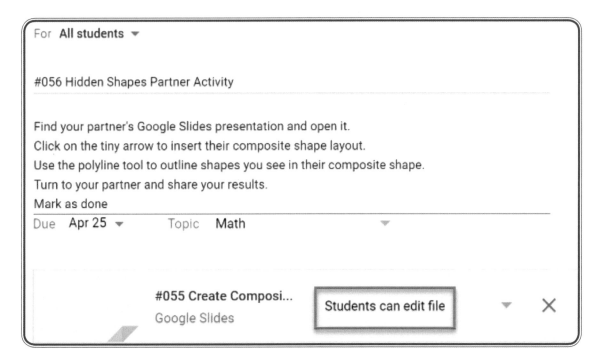

When students are in their partner's activity, they can add the composite shape layout into their filmstrip and find shapes within the composite shape. They can use the polyline tool to outline a shape. In doing so, the students need to make the fill color transparent, change the thickness of the borderline, and change the color of the line. By combining shapes, students can create a composite shape. This activity allows students to discover various shapes that develop the composite shape because multiple layouts can be inserted.

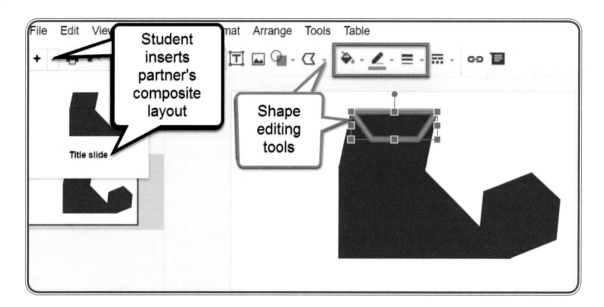

Template and Supporting Resources

Blank Google Slides Template:
alicekeeler.com/blankslides

Partner Activity on Composite Shapes Lesson Plan:
alicekeeler.com/compositepartners

Composite Shapes Partner Activity Directions for Littles:
christinepinto.com/compositepartnerdirections

Reason with Shapes

Students can add their own piece to a structured lesson. In the "Reason with Shapes" template, students start out by partitioning a pie on a Google Slide. Students click on the *Shape* icon to reveal the menu that has options for inserting a line. They can explain how they sliced the pie on the right side.

Partition the pie. Use the line tool to draw lines to cut the pie. Explain how you cut it up.

I partitioned the pie in eighths. I cut the pie in half, then half again, and two diagonal pieces. I did it this way so it would have even pieces for a lot of people to eat

Inserting a line in Google Slides can be done by clicking on the *Insert* menu and selecting *Line* or by clicking on the *Line* icon in the toolbar. When a line is selected (outlined in blue), the line color, thickness, and style can be changed. These tools are helpful for students to make their lines or partitions stand out above the image.

insert line

line color

line thickness

line dash

Students can then insert a slide layout that calls for them to insert an image of their choice and to partition it. They will have to think about what they are going to cut up, how they are going to cut it up, and why they would cut it up in the first place. This activity beats a worksheet where students are given images and shapes to cut up because the kids are choosing their own images, and it requires them to describe their thinking and demonstrate the different ways items can be partitioned.

Template

Reason with Shapes:
alicekeeler.com/reasonwithshapes

Explain what shape you cut up and describe the pieces.

I cut up a rectangular prism into 4 pieces and then 6 pieces. There are 24 pieces. I did not cut the pieces too small so people get a good size piece of cake.

House Hunters

Using technology opens the window to do things that previously were impossible or difficult. Much of the traditional math curriculum—textbooks and worksheets—uses numbers that are fictitious or made up. For example, "Johnny carried forty watermelons." Who is Johnny and where did these forty watermelons come from? With the Internet, you have a plethora of real data that can be used to provide students with more authentic learning experiences.

Template

House Hunters Place Value Template:
alicekeeler.com/househunters

Rather than make up large numbers to have students identify place value, ask first or second grade students to go to a website such as realtor.com and choose four houses. Get students in the habit of making a choice and justifying it. Even if their rationale for picking a house was that it looks cozy, have them identify their reason. Students record in the spreadsheet the square footage and price of the house. They then recall for themselves the names of the place value and separate out the numbers by place value. If you use the "House Hunters Place Value" template, the formulas set up in the spreadsheet will allow the students to compare the numbers and have their answer checked.

	House Number	Square footage	Using your knowledge of place value, order the square footage of the 4 houses from least to greatest
Least	2	1103	Great job! These are in order from least to greatest
	1	1328	
	3	1400	
Greatest	4	1570	

Math Puzzles

Many math worksheets focus on low-level critical-thinking tasks, such as memorizing and following steps. Even Littles like a challenge, and they are completely capable of engaging in higher-order thinking. The website openmiddle.com provides examples of DOK 2 and DOK 3 math problems that can be adapted to use with G Suite. Upgrading the activity with technology allows for collaboration and creativity. The possibility for faster feedback is also a benefit of G Suite. Using a spreadsheet, conditional formatting can be used to check student answers. Students receive immediate feedback, which can be very motivating.

In the "Number Puzzle—Addition and Subtraction within 20" template, Littles work toward solving problems involving addition and subtraction. In the "Sums and Differences within 20" spreadsheet puzzle, which was inspired by Jonathan Robinson (mr-mathematics.com), students try out numbers in the yellow boxes to solve the puzzle. This requires strategic thinking, DOK 3, rather than simply finding sums and differences, which is DOK 1. There are four puzzles in the spreadsheet. Two are addition and two are subtraction. When all four of the sum or difference boxes turn green, the student has solved the puzzle. We suggest deleting or hiding the *Directions* and the *Auto Gen New Puzzles* tabs before distributing a copy to students through Google Classroom.

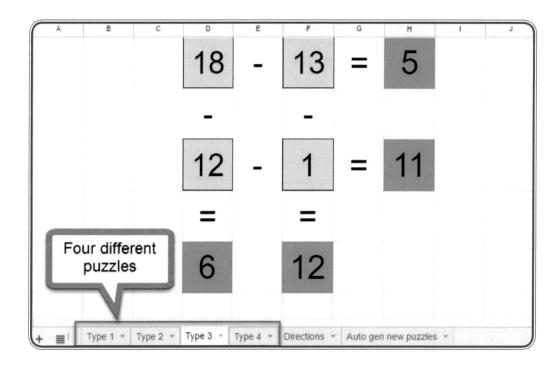

Template

Number Puzzle—Addition and Subtraction within 20:
alicekeeler.com/mathpuzzle20

Learn More

Additional books to support math instruction:

Teaching Math with Google Apps
by Alice Keeler and Diana Herrington:
alicekeeler.com/googlemath

***Instant Relevance* by Denis Sheeran:**
christinepinto.com/instantrelevance

***The Classroom Chef* by John Stevens and Matt Vaudrey:**
christinepinto.com/classroomchef

***Table Talk Math* by John Stevens (great for parents too):**
christinepinto.com/tabletalkmath

Chapter 9
Personalizing Feedback

My (Pinto) favorite way to give feedback to students is when they are right in front of me, in person. Real-time feedback *does not* disappear with technology in the classroom. Technology gives us *another* way for teachers to provide feedback to students. Work becomes more meaningful for students when they know someone is taking a close look at it and responding to it, whether it be their peers, their parents, or even a class that is connecting from a different region. Other means of digital feedback are available, beyond what needs to be read, and can add a personal touch. Many primary students are learning how to read. Fortunately, visual feedback such as using Bitmoji images and video responses are options for ways we can leave feedback for our Littles' digital work.

Accessing Student Work

Teachers have access to students' digital work completed in Google Apps through Google Classroom and Google Drive. In the Classroom stream, click on the assignment link. Information about which students have *Done* and *Not done* the assignment will appear. You can click on the individual tiles to view student work or click on the folder icon, which will open in Google Drive.

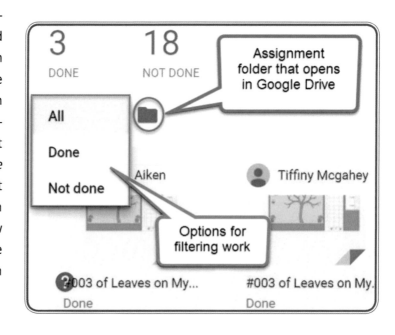

Drive20

Opening up each student's file would take a lot of time, a lot of clicking, and a lot of keeping track of whose assignment you have already seen. The Drive20 Chrome extension solves those issues and makes this tedious task effortless. Drive20 allows you to open all of the files inside the assignment folder at the same time. Each assignment gets opened up in a new tab. This makes it easy to view student work, give feedback, close the tab, and move on to the next student.

Learn More

Drive20 Chrome Extension:
tinyurl.com/drive20

Details about setting up Drive20:
alicekeeler.com/drive20

Bitmoji in Google Apps

If some students are not reading yet, you can still provide visual feedback by dragging a Bitmoji image from the Bitmoji Chrome Extension in Google Slides, Drawing, and Docs. Adding your Bitmoji to students' work gives a personal touch to your feedback; students can feel like you are interacting with them.

Learn More

Bitmoji Chrome Extension:
bit.ly/2q5lNb6

Bitmoji in Slides and Drawings

First add the Bitmoji Chrome Extension to your Chrome browser. It will appear in the area next to the Omnibox, or the web address bar. Click on the Bitmoji icon to reveal your options. Then simply drag a Bitmoji image into the Google App of your student's work.

In Google Slides and Google Drawing, the Bitmoji image can be placed in the gray canvas area and can be moved with ease.

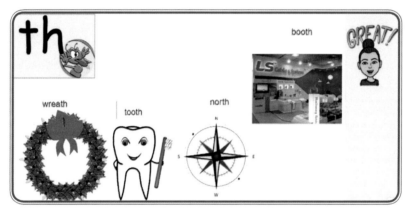

Bitmoji in Docs

In Google Docs, the Bitmoji image cannot be placed on the side and needs to be placed into the body of the document. Create a table where you want to place your Bitmoji. When you are designing a template for your students, you can place the table in the Google Doc before you assign the activity in Google Classroom. Anticipate where students' responses will be and include a table cell for their response and a cell for your Bitmoji image. For example, a 2x1 table will allow students to respond on the left cell and the Bitmoji image to go in the right cell.

You can erase the table lines for you Bitmoji feedback table by right clicking and selecting *Table properties*. Change the border to a width of zero. Should you ever have a template in which you wanted kids to fill in an answer within the Doc, you would insert a 1x1 table and have them type in the box.

Bitmoji in Forms

Unlike the other Google Apps, you cannot drag the Bitmoji image into Forms. In Google Forms, click on the image icon and select *By URL*. When using the Bitmoji Chrome extension, you can right click on the Bitmoji and select *Copy image address*. Paste it (using *Control-V* or *Command-V*) in Google Forms.

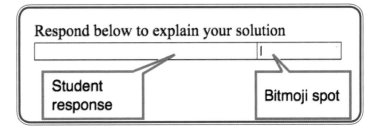

Learn More

Blog Post about Bitmoji in Google Docs:
alicekeeler.com/bitmojifeedback

Webcam Feedback

In Chapter 7, Alice offered a tip for recording a private comment for students. A video recording of yourself adds a very personal touch to feedback for students. Students can see and hear that you are speaking directly to them, even if you are not present. Saving the videos to Google Drive allows for easy insertion of the feedback video or link to the video.

Use the Alice Keeler Webcam Record Chrome extension to record with the webcam. The videos are automatically saved to Google Drive and the link to the video is automatically copied to the clipboard. Paste the link to the webcam feedback anywhere you would type comments. In Google Slides, use the *Insert* menu to add the video from Google Drive. This embeds the feedback right into the slide.

Students can also use the Webcam Record Chrome extension to give video submissions of answers. Students can insert the video responses into Google Slides. Be sure to help each student change the sharing permissions on the Webcam Record folder in Google Drive to *Anyone with the link can view.*

> ### Learn More
> **Alice Keeler Webcam Record:**
> alicekeeler.com/webcam

> ### Template
> **Alice Keeler Webcam Record Slides Template:**
> alicekeeler.com/webcamslides

Screencast Video Feedback

Screencasting is helpful when you want to refer to a student's work on a screen and include verbal feedback. Screencastify allows you to record in a current tab or desktop. Videos are saved in Google Drive and can be uploaded to YouTube. The tool is friendly enough for Littles to use as well, especially when they need to explain their thinking.

Videos are saved to a folder titled "Screencastify" in your Google Drive. Change the share settings on the folder to *Anyone with the link can view.* Include the

link from the Screencastify video in a comment in the student's Doc for the student to click on and view.

In Google Slides, videos can be inserted onto the actual slide. Use the *Insert* menu and select *Video*. You will be inserting the video from your Google Drive. Once the video is in the slide and is selected with the blue outline, click on *Video options* and check the box that says *Autoplay when presenting*. Students can click on the *Present* button to automatically play the video or can double click on the video camera icon to play the video and listen to the feedback.

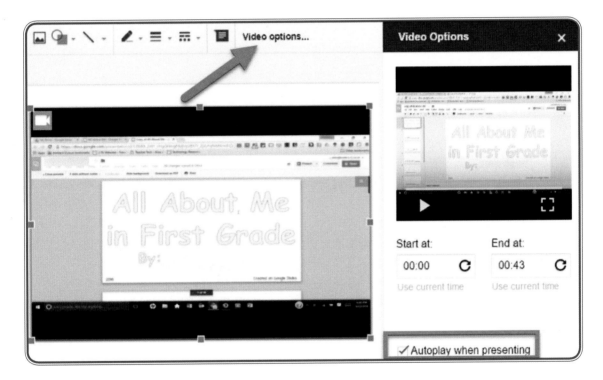

Recording a screencast and making it available for students also works well when providing audio and visual directions for students. Instead of having to repeat directions multiple times, or remind kids what to click on, they can refer to a directions video or a series of short clips. A tip to remember is to keep your videos short—think thirty seconds to one minute.

Learn More

Screencastify Chrome Extension:
christinepinto.com/screencastify

Chapter 10
G Suite for Teachers

Google Drive is your home base for Google Apps. It's where you will be able to create and save documents. You can access Google Drive at drive.google.com. It's also helpful to make Google Drive your homepage when you start up the Internet. Anything you create with Google Apps is automatically saved in Google Drive, and can be found there at a later time. The *New* button on the left-hand side of Google Drive allows you to create a new document, spreadsheet, slides presentation, or form.

Tip: Use Google Chrome when on a Chromebook, laptop, or PC to improve performance.

1. Create a Place for Collaboration

In education we *need* to share resources and ideas with our peers. The Google Apps platform makes sharing files and collaborating with colleagues simple. You can create a shared folder with your colleagues so you can have one place to keep those resources handy.

Start by selecting a folder and clicking on the share icon in the toolbar to share it with others. Any documents within that folder are automatically accessible to the people with whom you share it.

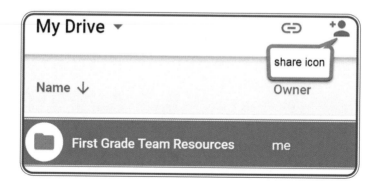

Team Drive

Creating your own folders and sharing them is one way to collaborate with specific people on your campus. Team Drive is similar to creating a folder in Google Drive, but it's intentionally designed for collaborating. If enabled by your G Suite administrator, you will be able to create a Team Drive as part of Google Drive. Simply click on Team Drives and add members via email address to the Drive. By default, members will have full access to the Drive, and it is advised to keep it that way when adding grade-level team members.

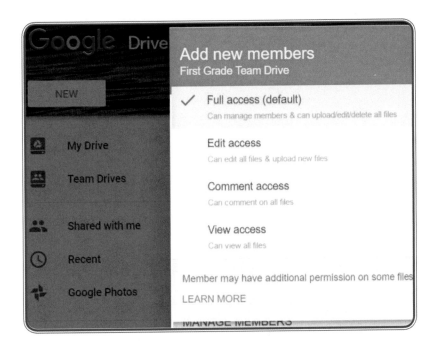

2. Collaborate on Lesson Planning

If you are lesson planning alone, you are working too hard. We all hold pieces of valuable information that become more meaningful when we put them together. Divide the workload! Plan lessons with your colleagues and even teachers outside your school who are part of your professional learning network. Twitter is a great place to connect with other educators, who often post their ideas and resources for free. You can meet people by searching for hashtags such as #kinderchat, #1stchat, #2ndchat, #gafe4littles, or #elemchat, and by following users who post on those hashtags.

Lesson plans should include information about the current learning standards, the four Cs—communication, collaboration, critical thinking, and creativity—and DOK, or depth of knowledge. The questions included in the "Collaborative Lesson Plan" template will get you and your learning network thinking about these elements, in addition to which Google tools you might include in your plan.

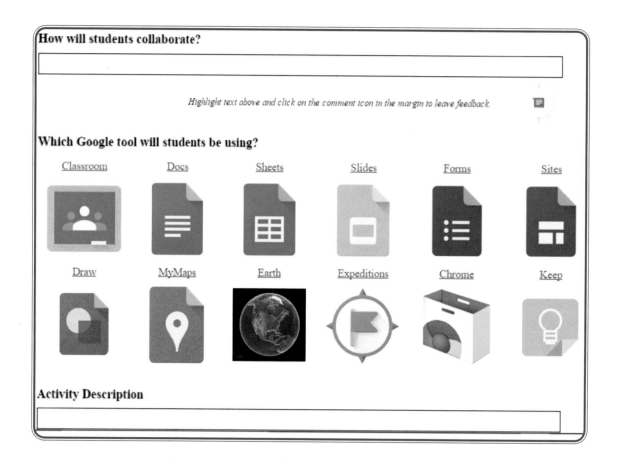

How will students collaborate?

Highlight text above and click on the comment icon in the margin to leave feedback.

Which Google tool will students be using?

| Classroom | Docs | Sheets | Slides | Forms | Sites |
| Draw | MyMaps | Earth | Expeditions | Chrome | Keep |

Activity Description

Template

Collaborative Lesson Plan:
alicekeeler.com/collablessonplan

Learn More

Directions for Sharing a Google Drive Folder:
alicekeeler.com/sharefolder

Getting Started with Team Drive:
goo.gl/blbyzK

G Suite Tips on Using Google Drive:
goo.gl/JepxDi

Google Drive Help for Sharing Folders:
goo.gl/lkgb1z

Google Drive Help:
goo.gl/pO9ssv

Details for Collaborative Lesson Plan Template:
alicekeeler.com/collabplandetails

Google Apps is excellent for sharing planning documents. Create a Google Doc or use Google Sheets to plan out activities with other teachers on your grade-level team. Collaborating with colleagues on Google Docs helps you to gain familiarity with the collaborative features of Google Apps. Through collaboration, you maximize the skill set of your grade-level team or professional learning network, which allows for new possibilities for student activities.

Notifications

When multiple teachers are collaborating for lesson planning, it is helpful to use the document notifications to alert each other to check or add to the planning document. Use the *File* menu and choose *Email collaborators*. This will send an email, along with a link, to those in the group.

Comment and Suggestion Modes

Comment and suggestion modes are additional ways to facilitate collaboration while planning lessons. Highlight a selection of text to comment on. Right click and choose *Comment* or use the comment icon that appears in the margin of a Google Text Document. As previously mentioned in Chapter 7, you can use the keyboard shortcut: *Control* (*Command* on a Mac), *Alt* (*Option* on a Mac), and *M* to insert a comment. Colleagues can click on the comment on the side to reply. This allows for the sharing of ideas to come to consensus even when you're unable to work on the file at the same time.

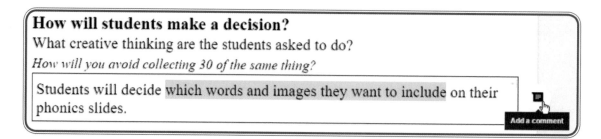

Suggestion mode allows collaborators to edit the text of a colleague without forcing the change. This allows for discussion around suggested edits.

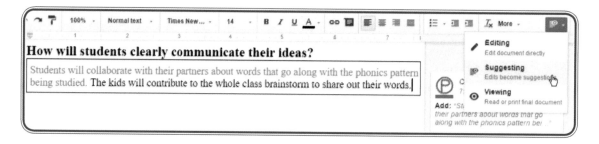

3. Create a Weekly Newsletter

Communication with students' families is essential. Sending home a weekly newsletter can keep parents informed about what is happening in the classroom. One great organization tip is to create a folder to hold all of your weekly newsletters. That way they are all in one place. Then draft your newsletter in Google Docs by going to docs.google.com.

Title Your Document

A new document in any Google app is untitled by default, which means you will need to title it. Click on the words *Untitled Document* in the upper left-hand corner of the screen and type in the title of your document.

Create Headings

When creating in Google Docs, the outline tool is helpful because it gives you headings options and auto-populates the outline as you update the document. Access the document outline by going to the *Tools* menu and selecting *Document outline*. The outline will appear to the left of the document. In the toolbar to the left of the font type, click on the small arrow where it says *Normal text* and select the heading type you think is appropriate for the section. Once you have your document complete, you can skip to any part of your document by clicking on one of the headers in the outline.

Template

Google Docs Sample Newsletter: christinepinto.com/weeklynewsletter

Share Past Newsletters

When parents are accustomed to receiving your newsletters, chances are a mom or dad might want to read one from an earlier week. Using the "List of Newsletters" template, you can create a list of previous newsletters in a spreadsheet, and share the link of the spreadsheet with parents.

After obtaining your copy of the "Share Past Newsletters" template, locate the add-on menu in the spreadsheet and click on *List of newsletters* and *Start*. Allow the prompt that asks for permission to access the necessary data. Then follow the next prompt guiding you to single click on the folder that contains your newsletters.

A list of the newsletters from the selected folder will generate into the spreadsheet. The purpose of Column A is to write a brief note about the newsletter. As you create weekly newsletters week after week, you can use the *Update files* feature, which will add those Docs to the list in the spreadsheet.

Share the link to the spreadsheet with parents by clicking on the blue *Share* button. Be sure to have the spreadsheet on *Anyone with the link can view*. Click on the *Copy link* button and paste it into an email or wherever you are going to communicate to the parents about the list of newsletters. From your newsletter spreadsheet, parents will be able to click on the link to any newsletter they would like to revisit.

Template

List of Newsletters: alicekeeler.com/listofnewsletters

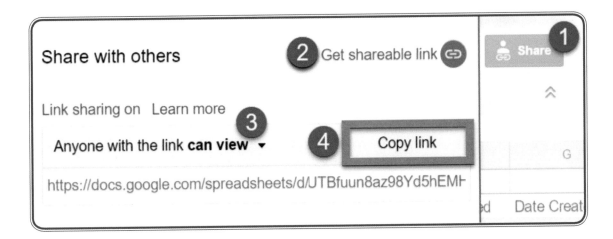

4. Create a Classroom Volunteer Form

Using paper limits your reach to parents. Paper forms get lost in transit. Parents intend to fill out forms, but things happen and the form may or may not make it back to your classroom. Reading parent handwriting can also be challenging. The bottom line is that communicating via paper can be a mess.

Using a Google Form to collect information allows busy parents to contribute from their mobile devices. Parents do not need to log in or have a Google Account to fill out the form. Be aware that your form might have a default setting that restricts its use to users at your school or on your domain. Just click on the icon in Google Forms to uncheck the restriction.

Google Forms collects responses all in one place, making it easy to manage information. Choosing to create a spreadsheet for the form provides a single list of all the parent responses. This information can no longer be lost, and both the form and the spreadsheet are located in Google Drive, accessible from any device connected to the Internet. In Google Drive you can search for forms and other documents to easily locate misplaced files. Try typing *volunteer* into the search box in Drive to bring up your volunteer Form.

Here's a quick guide to creating a Google Form:

- Title the form.
- Add questions from the floating toolbar.
- Select the question type that best represents the type of question you are asking.
- Click on the *Responses* tab to create a spreadsheet to collect responses to the form.

What email address can I contact you with in regards to volunteering? *

Your answer

Please check any of the following that you would be interested in helping with. *

☐ I would like to help with prepping activities: cutting, copying, and pasting.

☐ I would like to donate supplies, books, snacks, etc.

☐ I would like to help during center time (8:30-9:30 AM)

☐ I would like to share a special talent or occupation (please identify below)

☐ Other:

Template

Sample Volunteer Google Form:
christinepinto.com/volunteerform

Learn More

Directions for Creating a Volunteer Google Form:
christinepinto.com/createvolunteerform

Timestamp	Your child's name	Your name	What email address can I contact you with in regards to volunteering?	Please check any of the following that you would be interested in helping with.	If you are able to help during center time, what days are you available to volunteer?
8/30/2017	Bryan Jimenez	Sandra Jimenez	sandraj77@email.com	I would like to help with prepping activities: cutting, copying, and pasting., I would like to donate supplies, books, snacks, etc.	
8/30/2017	Frank Gemo	Robert Gemo	mrgemo@email.com	I would like to help during center time (8:30-9:30 AM)	Wednesday
8/31/2017	Sarah Lan	Amy Lan	alan@email.com	I would like to help during center time (8:30-9:30 AM)	Monday, Tuesday, Wednesday

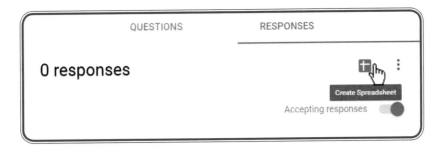

Now you're ready to share your Google Form. There are many settings and features within Google Forms, and the best way to learn is to click on all of the various icons, menus, and buttons. You learn a new tool by clicking around and exploring it. Look for icons of three stacked dots, three horizontal lines, or a tiny triangle to view more options for customizing.

5. Create Thinking Maps

Teachers can use Google Slides to support instruction by providing visuals for their students, posting a schedule or directions, or designing digital activities. Chart paper is traditionally used to create resources such as thinking maps, word family lists, and sentence frames. After the materials are created, the posters are displayed in the classroom. If you are lucky enough to have the space in your classroom, they stay up all year. There are also many benefits to creating thinking maps and posters in Google Slides, especially if you create all of them in the same presentation. Here are a few ways to use these resources:

- **Put it on the big screen**: The slide you create your poster on can be displayed on the whiteboard to support students during an assignment.

- **Print out a few copies**: Multiple copies can be printed out for small groups to allow closer viewing access. Because the slides print out on letter-size paper and are smaller than the typical poster, it is feasible to dedicate a bulletin board or cabinet area and display the posters all year.

- **Share in Google Classroom**: Assign the link to the slides in Google Classroom or post the link in the *About* tab for students to access whenever they are working in their Google accounts.

- **Share with parents**: The link to the slides can be shared with parents via email or a class website so students can access them at home and parents can see what type of learning is happening in the classroom.

- **Model your process for students:** If you choose to create the thinking map or poster in real time (while you put the kids' ideas on the slide), talk through the steps. Narrate what you are clicking on and how you are inserting, formatting, and backspacing. The kids will eventually be creating their own resources and thinking maps from scratch, and it helps for them to see and become familiar with the pattern of formatting.

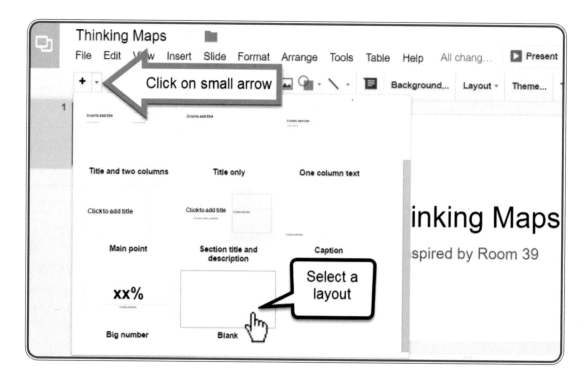

Access Google Slides by going to slides.google.com and clicking on a new presentation. Have the first slide be your title slide, and then insert a blank layout. Google Slides comes with premade layouts. Click on the small arrow next to the printer icon to reveal them. Working on the blank layout will let you create from scratch. Use the *Insert* menu to insert a text box. Format the text box by using the toolbar to edit as you wish. Continue to insert more text boxes to develop your thinking map.

Tip: If you have a text box formatted and you need duplicates of it, use the keyboard shortcut *Control-D* (*Command-D* on a Mac) while the text box is selected in blue. This will duplicate the text box and you can drag it where you need it.

There is no need to recreate a thinking map every time you need a new one. Just duplicate the slide. In the filmstrip area, click on the slide you would like to duplicate. In the *Slide* menu, click *Duplicate slide*. Alternatively, you can use the *Control-D* keyboard shortcut to duplicate the slide.

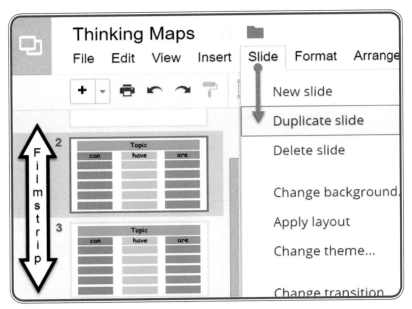

Template

Thinking Map Layouts: christinepinto.com/thinkingmaps

6. Create a Class Roster

Having an easily accessible class roster is important. Class rosters can be used to keep track of who has turned in field trip permission slips, put kids in a height order for a performance, record individual observations, and more. It's also a helpful tool to include in an emergency bag.

To create a class roster, you need to enter the students' names into a table, and Google Sheets is just the Google App for that task. To create a new spreadsheet, go to sheets.google.com.

Give your spreadsheet a title in the upper-left-hand corner. In a spreadsheet, you can format all of the cells at the same time by clicking on the *Awesome Box*, which selects all of the cells in the spreadsheet. The bars next to the Awesome Box are called the *freeze bars*. You can click on either the horizontal or vertical freeze bar underneath a row or column of cells and they will not move as you navigate through your spreadsheet.

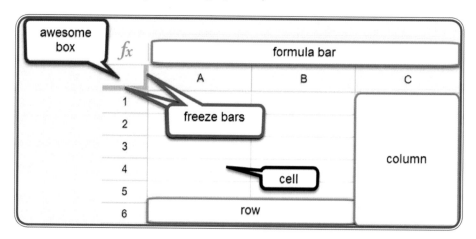

Start off by titling your columns. Assign your students a class number, and put the number in column A. Columns B and C can be for first and last names. Drag the horizontal freeze bar underneath row 1. Type students' first names in column B and last names in column C. Names can be sorted in alphabetical order by clicking on the filter arrow icon in either of the columns.

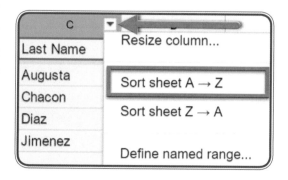

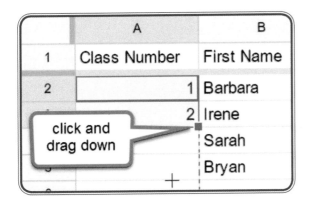

After student names are sorted to your liking, number your students. Class numbers are helpful when labeling items in the classroom, organizing or sorting papers, and lining up for safety drills. Spreadsheets are awesome because they can do a lot for you automatically—it just takes some formatting on your part. Instead of typing each number for each child, you can start typing the first few numbers, holding the *Shift* key to select the cells with the numbers, and clicking and dragging the blue corner of your selection down the column. After you have entered names and class numbers, your roster is complete.

Don't forget to duplicate it! Instead of having multiple Google Sheet documents of the various types of lists, it's easy to keep all of them in one document. By default, the first sheet in Google Sheets is titled Sheet 1. At the bottom of the spreadsheet, double click on the sheet tab and retitle it Master Sheet. Click the tiny triangle on the sheet tab to duplicate the master list. Every time you duplicate the master sheet, rename the new sheet. You can continue to duplicate the master roster list as needed throughout the year, while keeping all of your sheets in one spreadsheet.

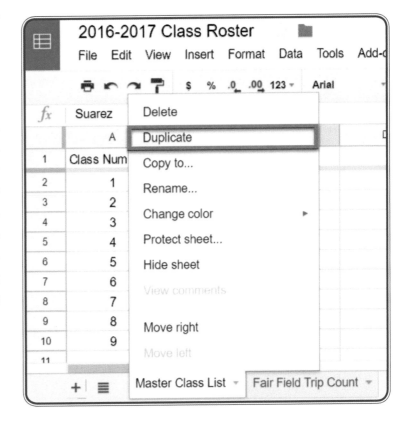

7. Tools for Publishing

Anyone Can View

Google tools provide a variety of opportunities for students to produce and publish their own writing. Digital work in Google text documents or Google Slides, for example, can easily be shared with parents or other audiences.

When you want to share student work, it is important to be aware of the document's sharing settings. Documents created in G Suite are, by default, private. Sharing the link to the document will result in the viewer getting a permissions error. When students share a document in Google Classroom, this automatically provides editing permissions to the teacher but no one else. To allow parents or others to view the document, students must use the blue *Share* button to change the permissions.

Knowing how to share a document is an essential skill. When students are aware of how a document is shared, they can use the Chrome extension AnyoneCanView. With one click, the document permissions are changed to *Anyone with the link can view*, allowing others outside of the domain, who have the link, to view the document. The exception to this will be if the G Suite apps administrator has restricted sharing to the domain, in which case files cannot be shared with anyone, including parents, outside of the school accounts.

Learn More

AnyoneCanView Chrome extension:
alicekeeler.com/anyone

Information about Various Share Settings:
alicekeeler.com/sharesettings

Publish to the Web

To create a professional preview of their documents, students can use the *File* menu and choose *Publish to the web*. A link is provided that displays the document like a webpage without the editing and formatting toolbars. The *Publish to the web* option also provides an embed code so student work can easily be displayed within a webpage, such as your class blog.

Students can skip knowing how to use an embed code if they are using Google Sites to publish their work, because double clicking in Google Sites brings up a menu to insert Google documents from Google Drive.

ePubs

Another way to publish student work is to create an ePub. Google Docs offers the choice to download a file as an ePub publication. This allows the document to be viewed on an e-reader or mobile device. An ePub can also be used to publish to digital book websites such as Amazon.

Conclusion

Our driving message in *Google Apps for Littles* centers on *believing*. Believe in yourself, that you can integrate a new learning platform with your young students. Believe in your students, that they will thrive with Google Apps and other technologies as learning and creating tools. We have shared tips and ideas in this book, but the very first step for you is to believe that integrating Google Apps is possible for your students.

We understand that using technology in this way may involve some risk-taking and stepping out of your comfort zone. Sometimes I tell my kids, "We are going to try something new today, and Miss Pinto has no idea how it will turn out, but we are going to be brave and explore together, and try!" A lot of the time, things go well, and other times, we need to regroup and move forward.

Our youngest learners deserve opportunities to create and discover with technology. Know that you are not alone on this adventure with your students. Join the community of teachers and student advocates on the #GAfE4Littles hashtag on Twitter, where many connect and share about the adventures they are taking with their students and technology.

Thank You

To Shelley and Dave Burgess for their patience on the completion of the book and for supporting the message behind #GAfE4Littles.

From Christine Pinto

To my spring transitional kindergarten class of 2016 and kindergarten class of 2017, who fearlessly explored new learning horizons with me; in addition to their parents for their support throughout the school year and consent to include photographs and samples of their children's work.

To the administration and my fellow colleagues at Arcadia Unified School District for welcoming my ideas and valuing innovation and collaboration.

From Alice Keeler

To my wonderful creative children Reagan, Jackson, Nixon, Keaton Atari (who goes by Bacon), and W, who constantly inspire me with what they are able to do with technology.

To my Twitter PLN, who daily make me a better educator. Thank you for sharing your ideas that inspire so much of what I know about using technology with Littles. Thank you for trying out the ideas and templates with your Littles! Follow #GAfE4Littles on Twitter to join in the conversation.

To the Google for Education team, who listens to teachers when creating products and supports so many educators with free tools that make learning better for our Littles.

A special thank you to the following educators for their ideas in the book:

Michelle Baldwin, Hans Tullmann, Lisa Highfill, Kelly Hilton, Sarah Landis, James Sanders, Adam Bellow, Kasey Bell, Jonathan Robinson, Bryan Anderson, John Ulbright, Robert Kaplinsky, Cori Orlando, and Bob Smith.

More from Dave Burgess Consulting, Inc.

Teach Like a PIRATE

Increase Student Engagement, Boost Your Creativity, and Transform Your Life as an Educator

By Dave Burgess (@BurgessDave)

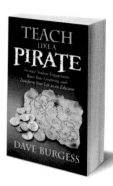

   Teach Like a PIRATE is the New York Times' best-selling book that has sparked a worldwide educational revolution. It is part inspirational manifesto that ignites passion for the profession and part practical road map, filled with dynamic strategies to dramatically increase student engagement. Translated into multiple languages, its message resonates with educators who want to design outrageously creative lessons and transform school into a life-changing experience for students.

Learn Like a PIRATE

Empower Your Students to Collaborate, Lead, and Succeed

By Paul Solarz (@PaulSolarz)

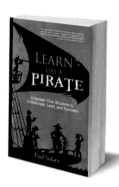

   Today's job market demands that students be prepared to take responsibility for their lives and careers. We do them a disservice if we teach them how to earn passing grades without equipping them to take charge of their education. In *Learn Like a PIRATE*, Paul Solarz explains how to design classroom experiences that encourage students to take risks and explore their passions in a stimulating, motivating, and supportive environment where improvement, rather than grades, is the focus. Discover how student-led classrooms help students thrive and develop into self-directed, confident citizens who are capable of making smart, responsible decisions, all on their own.

P is for PIRATE

Inspirational ABC's for Educators

By Dave and Shelley Burgess (@Burgess_Shelley)

   Teaching is an adventure that stretches the imagination and calls for creativity every day! In *P is for PIRATE*, husband and wife team Dave and Shelley Burgess encourage and inspire educators to make their classrooms fun and exciting places to learn. Tapping into years of personal experience and drawing on the insights of more than seventy educators, the authors offer a wealth of ideas for making learning and teaching more fulfilling than ever before.

Play Like a Pirate

Engage Students with Toys, Games, and Comics. Make Your Classroom Fun Again!

By Quinn Rollins (@jedikermit)

Yes! School can be simultaneously fun and educational. In *Play Like a Pirate*, Quinn Rollins offers practical, engaging strategies and resources that make it easy to integrate fun into your curriculum. Regardless of the grade level you teach, you'll find inspiration and ideas that will help you engage your students in unforgettable ways.

eXPlore Like a Pirate

Gamification and Game-Inspired Course Design to Engage, Enrich, and Elevate Your Learners

By Michael Matera (@MrMatera)

Are you ready to transform your classroom into an experiential world that flourishes on collaboration and creativity? Then set sail with classroom game designer and educator Michael Matera as he reveals the possibilities and power of game-based learning. In *eXPlore Like a Pirate*, Matera serves as your experienced guide to help you apply the most motivational techniques of gameplay to your classroom. You'll learn gamification strategies that will work with and enhance (rather than replace) your current curriculum and discover how these engaging methods can be applied to any grade level or subject.

The Innovator's Mindset

Empower Learning, Unleash Talent, and Lead a Culture of Creativity

By George Couros (@gcouros)

The traditional system of education requires students to hold their questions and compliantly stick to the scheduled curriculum. But our job as educators is to provide new and better opportunities for our students. It's time to recognize that compliance doesn't foster innovation, encourage critical thinking, or inspire creativity—and those are the skills our students need to succeed. In *The Innovator's Mindset*, George Couros encourages teachers and administrators to empower their learners to wonder, to explore—and to become forward-thinking leaders.

Master the Media

How Teaching Media Literacy Can Save Our Plugged-in World

By Julie Smith (@julnilsmith)

Written to help teachers and parents educate the next generation, *Master the Media* explains the history, purpose, and messages behind the media. The point isn't to get kids to unplug; it's to help them make informed choices, understand the difference between truth and lies, and discern perception from reality. Critical thinking leads to smarter decisions—and it's why media literacy can save the world.

The Zen Teacher

Creating FOCUS, SIMPLICITY, and TRANQUILITY in the Classroom

By Dan Tricarico (@TheZenTeacher)

Teachers have incredible power to influence—even improve—the future. In *The Zen Teacher*, educator, blogger, and speaker Dan Tricarico provides practical, easy-to-use techniques to help teachers be their best—unrushed and fully focused—so they can maximize their performance and improve their quality of life. In this introductory guide, Dan Tricarico explains what it means to develop a Zen practice—something that has nothing to do with religion and everything to do with your ability to thrive in the classroom.

Lead Like a PIRATE

Make School Amazing for Your Students and Staff

By Shelley Burgess and Beth Houf (@Burgess_Shelley, @BethHouf)

In *Lead Like a PIRATE*, education leaders Shelley Burgess and Beth Houf map out the character traits necessary to captain a school or district. You'll learn where to find the treasure that's already in your classrooms and schools—and how to bring out the very best in your educators. This book will equip and encourage you to be relentless in your quest to make school amazing for your students, staff, parents, and communities.

50 Things You Can Do with Google Classroom

By Alice Keeler and Libbi Miller (@AliceKeeler, @MillerLibbi)

It can be challenging to add new technology to the classroom, but it's a must if students are going to be well-equipped for the future. Alice Keeler and Libbi Miller shorten the learning curve by providing a thorough overview of the Google Classroom App. Part of Google Apps for Education (GAfE), Google Classroom was specifically designed to help teachers save time by streamlining the process of going digital. Complete with screenshots, *50 Things You Can Do with Google Classroom* provides ideas and step-by-step instructions to help teachers implement this powerful tool.

50 Things to Go Further with Google Classroom

A Student-Centered Approach

By Alice Keeler and Libbi Miller (@AliceKeeler, @MillerLibbi)

Today's technology empowers educators to move away from the traditional classroom where teachers lead and students work independently—each doing the same thing. In *50 Things to Go Further with Google Classroom: A Student-Centered Approach*, authors and educators Alice Keeler and Libbi Miller offer inspiration and resources to help you create a digitally rich, engaging, student-centered environment. They show you how to tap into the power of individualized learning that is possible with Google Classroom.

Pure Genius

Building a Culture of Innovation and Taking 20% Time to the Next Level

By Don Wettrick (@DonWettrick)

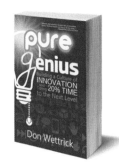

For far too long, schools have been bastions of boredom, killers of creativity, and way too comfortable with compliance and conformity. In *Pure Genius*, Don Wettrick explains how collaboration—with experts, students, and other educators—can help you create interesting, and even life-changing, opportunities for learning. Wettrick's book inspires and equips educators with a systematic blueprint for teaching innovation in any school.

140 Twitter Tips for Educators

Get Connected, Grow Your Professional Learning Network, and Reinvigorate Your Career

By Brad Currie, Billy Krakower, and Scott Rocco
(@bradmcurrie, @wkrakower, @ScottRRocco)

Whatever questions you have about education or about how you can be even better at your job, you'll find ideas, resources, and a vibrant network of professionals ready to help you on Twitter. In *140 Twitter Tips for Educators,* #Satchat hosts and founders of Evolving Educators, Brad Currie, Billy Krakower, and Scott Rocco, offer step-by-step instructions to help you master the basics of Twitter, build an online following, and become a Twitter rock star.

Ditch That Textbook

Free Your Teaching and Revolutionize Your Classroom

By Matt Miller (@jmattmiller)

Textbooks are symbols of centuries-old education. They're often outdated as soon as they hit students' desks. Acting "by the textbook" implies compliance and a lack of creativity. It's time to ditch those textbooks—and those textbook assumptions about learning! In *Ditch That Textbook*, teacher and blogger Matt Miller encourages educators to throw out meaningless, pedestrian teaching and learning practices. He empowers them to evolve and improve on old, standard teaching methods. *Ditch That Textbook* is a support system, toolbox, and manifesto to help educators free their teaching and revolutionize their classrooms.

How Much Water Do We Have?

5 Success Principles for Conquering Any Challenge and Thriving in Times of Change

by Pete Nunweiler with Kris Nunweiler

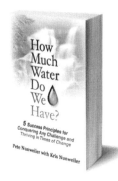

In *How Much Water Do We Have?* Pete Nunweiler identifies five key elements—information, planning, motivation, support, and leadership—that are necessary for the success of any goal, life transition, or challenge. Referring to these elements as the 5 Waters of Success, Pete explains that, like the water we drink, you need them to thrive in today's rapidly paced world. If you're feeling stressed out, overwhelmed, or uncertain at work or at home, pause and look for the signs of dehydration. Learn how to find, acquire, and use the 5 Waters of Success—so you can share them with your team and family members.

Instant Relevance

Using Today's Experiences to Teach Tomorrow's Lessons

By Denis Sheeran (@MathDenisNJ)

Every day, students in schools around the world ask the question, "When am I ever going to use this in real life?" In *Instant Relevance*, author and keynote speaker Denis Sheeran equips you to create engaging lessons *from* experiences and events that matter to your students. Learn how to help your students see meaningful connections between the real world and what they learn in the classroom—because that's when learning sticks.

The Classroom Chef

Sharpen Your Lessons. Season Your Classes. Make Math Meaningful.

By John Stevens and Matt Vaudrey (@Jstevens009, @MrVaudrey)

In *The Classroom Chef*, math teachers and instructional coaches John Stevens and Matt Vaudrey share their secret recipes, ingredients, and tips for serving up lessons that engage students and help them "get" math. You can use these ideas and methods as-is, or better yet, tweak them and create your own enticing educational meals. The message the authors share is that, with imagination and preparation, every teacher can be a classroom chef.

Start. Right. Now.

Teach and Lead for Excellence

By Todd Whitaker, Jeff Zoul, and Jimmy Casas
(@ToddWhitaker, @Jeff_Zoul, @casas_jimmy)

In their work leading up to *Start. Right. Now.*, Todd Whitaker, Jeff Zoul, and Jimmy Casas studied educators from across the nation and discovered four key behaviors of excellence: Excellent leaders and teachers *Know the Way, Show the Way, Go the Way, and Grow Each Day*. If you are ready to take the first step toward excellence, this motivating book will put you on the right path.

The Writing on the Classroom Wall

How Posting Your Most Passionate Beliefs about Education Can Empower Your Students, Propel Your Growth, and Lead to a Lifetime of Learning

By Steve Wyborney (@SteveWyborney)

In *The Writing on the Classroom Wall*, Steve Wyborney explains how posting and discussing Big Ideas can lead to deeper learning. You'll learn why sharing your ideas will sharpen and refine them. You'll also be encouraged to know that the Big Ideas you share don't have to be profound to make a profound impact on learning. In fact, Steve explains, it's okay if some of your ideas fall *off* the wall. What matters most is sharing them.

LAUNCH

Using Design Thinking to Boost Creativity and Bring Out the Maker in Every Student

By John Spencer and A.J. Juliani (@spencerideas, @ajjuliani)

Something happens in students when they define themselves as *makers* and *inventors* and *creators*. They discover powerful skills—problem-solving, critical thinking, and imagination—that will help them shape the world's future ... *our* future. In *LAUNCH*, John Spencer and A.J. Juliani provide a process that can be incorporated into every class at every grade level ... even if you don't consider yourself a "creative teacher." And if you dare to innovate and view creativity as an essential skill, you will empower your students to change the world—starting right now.

Kids Deserve It!

Pushing Boundaries and Challenging Conventional Thinking

By Todd Nesloney and Adam Welcome (@TechNinjaTodd, @awelcome)

In *Kids Deserve It!*, Todd and Adam encourage you to think big and make learning fun and meaningful for students. Their high-tech, high-touch, and highly engaging practices will inspire you to take risks, shake up the status quo, and be a champion for your students. While you're at it, you just might rediscover why you became an educator in the first place.

Escaping the School Leader's Dunk Tank

How to Prevail When Others Want to See You Drown

By Rebecca Coda and Rick Jetter (@RebeccaCoda, @RickJetter)

No school leader is immune to the effects of discrimination, bad politics, revenge, or ego-driven coworkers. These kinds of dunk-tank situations can make an educator's life miserable. By sharing real-life stories and insightful research, the authors (who are dunk-tank survivors themselves) equip school leaders with the practical knowledge and emotional tools necessary to survive and, better yet, avoid getting "dunked."

Teaching Math with Google Apps

50 G Suite Activities

By Alice Keeler and Diana Herrington (@AliceKeeler, @mathdiana)

Google Apps give teachers the opportunity to interact with students in a more meaningful way than ever before, while G Suite empowers students to be creative, critical thinkers who collaborate as they explore and learn. In *Teaching Math with Google Apps*, educators Alice Keeler and Diana Herrington demonstrate fifty different ways to bring math classes to the twenty-first century with easy-to-use technology.

Your School Rocks ... So Tell People!

Passionately Pitch and Promote the Positives Happening on Your Campus

By Ryan McLane and Eric Lowe (@McLane_Ryan, @EricLowe21)

Great things are happening in your school every day. The problem is, no one beyond your school walls knows about them. School principals Ryan McLane and Eric Lowe want to help you get the word out! In *Your School Rocks ... So Tell People!*, McLane and Lowe offer more than seventy immediately actionable tips along with easy-to-follow instructions and links to video tutorials. This practical guide will equip you to create an effective and manageable communication strategy using social media tools. Learn how to keep your students' families and community connected, informed, and excited about what's going on in your school.

Table Talk Math

A Practical Guide for Bringing Math into Everyday Conversations

By John Stevens (@Jstevens009)

Making math part of families' everyday conversations is a powerful way to help children and teens learn to love math. In *Table Talk Math*, John Stevens offers parents (and teachers!) ideas for initiating authentic, math-based conversations that will get kids to notice and be curious about all the numbers, patterns, and equations in the world around them.

Shattering the Perfect Teacher Myth

6 Truths That Will Help You THRIVE as an Educator

By Aaron Hogan (@aaron_hogan)

The idyllic myth of the perfect teacher perpetuates unrealistic expectations that erode self-confidence and set teachers up for failure. Author and educator Aaron Hogan is on a mission to shatter the myth of the perfect teacher by equipping educators with strategies that help them shift out of survival mode and THRIVE.

Shift This!

How to Implement Gradual Changes for MASSIVE Impact in Your Classroom

By Joy Kirr (@JoyKirr)

Establishing a student-led culture that isn't focused on grades and homework but on individual responsibility and personalized learning may seem like a daunting task—especially if you think you have to do it all at once. But significant change is possible, sustainable, and even easy when it happens little by little. In *Shift This!* educator and speaker Joy Kirr explains how to make gradual shifts—in your thinking, teaching, and approach to classroom design—that will have a massive impact in your classroom. Make the first shift today!

Unmapped Potential

An Educator's Guide to Lasting Change

By Julie Hasson and Missy Lennard (@PPrincipals)

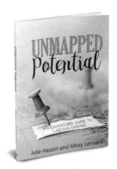

No matter where you are in your educational career, chances are you have, at times, felt overwhelmed and overworked. Maybe you feel that way right now. If so, you aren't alone. But the more important news is that things can get better! You simply need the right map to guide you from frustrated to fulfilled. *Unmapped Potential* offers advice and practical strategies to help you find your unique path to becoming the kind of educator—the kind of person—you want to be.

Social LEADia

Moving Students from Digital Citizenship to Digital Leadership

By Jennifer Casa-Todd (@JCasaTodd)

Equipping students for their future begins by helping them become digital leaders now. In our networked society, students need to learn how to leverage social media to connect to people, passions, and opportunities to grow and make a difference. *Social LEADia* addresses the need to shift the conversations at school and at home from digital citizenship to digital leadership.

Spark Learning

3 Keys to Embracing the Power of Student Curiosity

By Ramsey Musallam (@ramusallam)

Inspired by his popular TED Talk "3 Rules to Spark Learning," this book combines brain science research, proven teaching methods, and Ramsey's personal story to empower you to improve your students' learning experiences by inspiring inquiry and harnessing its benefits. If you want to engage students in more interesting and effective learning, this is the book for you.

Ditch That Homework

Practical Strategies to Help Make Homework Obsolete

By Matt Miller and Alice Keeler
(@jmattmiller, @alicekeeler)

In *Ditch That Homework*, Matt Miller and Alice Keeler discuss the pros and cons of homework, why teachers assign it, and what life could look like without it. As they evaluate the research and share parent and teacher insights, the authors offer a convincing case for ditching homework and replacing it with more effective and personalized learning methods.

The Four O'Clock Faculty

A Rogue Guide to Revolutionizing Professional Development

By Rich Czyz (@RACzyz)

Author Rich Czyz is on a mission to revolutionize professional learning for all educators. In *The Four O'Clock Faculty*, Rich identifies ways to make PD meaningful, efficient, and, above all, personally relevant. This book is a practical guide that reveals why some PD is so awful and what you can do to change the model for the betterment of you and your colleagues.

Culturize

Every Student. Every Day. Whatever It Takes.

By Jimmy Casas (@casas_jimmy)

In *Culturize*, author and education leader Jimmy Casas shares insights into what it takes to cultivate a community of learners who embody the innately human traits our world desperately needs, such as kindness, honesty, and compassion. His stories reveal how these "soft skills" can be honed while meeting and exceeding academic standards of twenty-first-century learning.

Code Breaker

Increase Creativity, Remix Assessment, and Develop a Class of Coder Ninjas!

By Brian Aspinall (@mraspinall)

Code Breaker equips you to use coding in your classroom to turn curriculum expectations into skills. Students learn how to identify problems, develop solutions, and use computational thinking to apply and demonstrate their learning. Best of all, you don't have to be a "computer geek" to empower your students with these essential skills.

The Wild Card

7 Steps to an Educator's Creative Breakthrough

By Hope and Wade King (@hopekingteach, @wadeking7)

Have you ever wished you were more creative . . . or that your students were more engaged in your lessons? *The Wild Card* is your step-by-step guide to experiencing a creative breakthrough in *your* classroom with your students. Wade and Hope King show you how to draw on your authentic self to deliver your content creatively and be the wild card who changes the game for your learners.

About the Authors

Christine Pinto

 @ pintobeanz11

I have been working with Littles since 2012. I grew up knowing that I wanted to work with kids in a positive environment, so I felt called to be a teacher. As soon as I started doing fieldwork hours for my child development courses, I knew that working with Littles would become my niche. I appreciate and enjoy their energy, excitement, and imagination. I value their open-mindedness toward school and strive to provide the best learning experiences for them. I am a strong believer that at the primary level kids can think critically and create amazing things.

While working on my master's degree, I studied technology integration in early childhood education and was disappointed with the lack of variety in activities for Littles using technology. At the same time, I was teaching my first class and felt compelled to take my kids further with their learning skills and explore more with technology. I began sharing what my students were doing on Twitter and founded the #GAfE4Littles hashtag, which stands for Google Apps for Education for Littles. #GAfE4Littles is a growing network of educators and advocates who share stories and resources to help Littles succeed. Connect with me on Twitter, @pintobeanz11, and stay current with the newest resources I share at christinepinto.com.

Alice Keeler

 @alicekeeler

Photo by Alex Kang / heyitsalex.com

I am a mom of five children. Technology permeates our house. Each of my children, even at a year old, amazed me with what they were able to do with technology and how they figured it out on their own. Rarely will they let me show them something—they got this. When my son was in second grade, I got him MineCraft. "Could I help you with this, son?" I asked. He replied, "No, I watched a few YouTube videos." Sadly, they go to school with all of this technology ability and lack of fear, and sometimes they are not given the opportunity to use it. "Mom, we have Chromebooks! Why can't we use them?" Don't let your inexperience with technology rob our students of the opportunity to express themselves digitally. Believe they can figure it out, that they can be creative with technology, and that they can teach you.

I taught high school math for fourteen years and was blessed to have been 1:1 the entire time. I have a bachelor's degree in mathematics and a master's degree in Educational Media Design and Technology. I'm a Google Certified Innovator, New Media Consortium Ambassador, and Microsoft Innovative Educator. I've served on the Horizon Report advisory committee since 2013. I'm currently teaching teachers in the credential program at California State University, Fresno. I have co-authored the books *50 Things You Can Do with Google Classroom*, *50 Things to Go Further with Google Classroom: A Student-Centered Approach*, *Teaching Math with Google Apps*, and *Ditch That Homework*.

Made in the USA
Lexington, KY
12 June 2019